LAKESHA DENISE

POWERFUL
Woman of Faith
Philippians 4:13

CoolBird Publishing House
THE AUTHOR'S NEST

Unless otherwise marked, all Scripture references are from the New King James Version of the Bible. Copyright ©1979, 1980, 1982 by Thomas Nelson, Inc. Published and used only as a reference. Scripture marked NIV, ESV, NKJV are taken from the New King James Version Copyright 1982 by Thomas Nelson, New International Version Copyright Zondervan online, English Standard Version Copyright Online are also only used as reference tools.

Powerful Woman of Faith: Philippians 4:13
Published by: CoolBird Publishing House
PO Box 612
Goodwater, AL 35072
www.coolbirdmarketing.com

This book or parts thereof may not be reproduced in any form, stored in a retrieval system, or transmitted in any form by any means-electronic, mechanical, photocopy, recording, or otherwise- without prior written permission of the publisher, except as provided by United States of America copyright law.

Copyright ©2018 by Lakesha Denise
All Rights Reserved.

ISBN: 978-1717365057
Published in the United States of America

The material contained in this book is provided for informational purposes only. It is not intended to diagnose, provide advice, or take the place of marital counseling from licensed professionals. Neither the publisher nor the author is responsible for any possible consequences from any person reading or following the information in this book.

Dedication

This book is dedicated to all my sisters in Christ who want to find faith and strength in their walk of struggles. Please know that through Jesus Christ you can conquer all obstacles.

POWERFUL
Woman of Faith
Philippians 4:13

TABLE OF CONTENTS

FOREWORD..	7
Chp 1 Lord, tell me why my marriage had to end?.................	13
Chp 2 Living with your choices...	36
Chp 3 The Boomerang...	48
Chp 4 Falling for The Representative..	64
Chp 5 Lord, tell me why does love hurt..................................	74
Chp 6 Single life is not for me..	88
Chp 7 Drowning in debt...	97
Chp 8 Someone prayed for me..	107
Chp 9 Repossession?..	116
Chp 10 Accepting your gift..	125
Chp 11 ADHD, Anxiety & Depression....................................	133
Chp 12 Raising kids..	147
Chp 13 Life's decisions..	159
Chp 14 Find who you are...	169
Chp 15 Worth..	177
Chp 16 Naked in Christ..	188
Chp 17 Under attack...	196
Chp 18 Time for yourself...	204

Acknowledgements

To my mom, Verlinda Thomas Young for always supporting me and letting me know that I'm a very strong woman and that I can accomplish all things through Christ.

To my kids, Jada Trimble and Trace Trimble, you are my gift from God. You have always been my motivators.

To my sister, Tawana Thomas thank you for encouraging me and always being in my corner.

To my brother, Demetrius Hoyett thank you for your guidance through life's situations with your faith.

To my family, thank you for always being there for me when I needed you without any hesitation.

To all the women and men that I have spoken with, thank you for trusting me to encourage, empower and pray for you. And, thank you for sharing your struggles in your journey and your heart's desires.

FOREWORD

When my sister blessed me with the pleasure to write the foreword in her first book, I didn't know if I would be able to...Not because I didn't want to, but simply because I was afraid that I was going to burst into tears. I witnessed her "rise from the ashes" as the Phoenix that she is. I first met Lakesha at my grandmother's house...She was hanging on the wall in a picture that her father had given my grandmother. It was her senior portrait. I met her face to face in 2007 at my ex-wife's baby shower. I was a true witness of how big her heart is because of what she did for our daughter. Lakesha's ability to overcome heartbreak, loss, and sadness showed what type of fighter she is. After my divorce in 2010, she opened her doors to me as a friend and allowed me to live with her and never made me feel like I was in her and her children's way. Even though she was living through her own hardship, this was just another example of her selfless heart. During that time, I saw tears of pain roll down her cheeks, but what I never saw was quitting. She would always say to me "Little brother, I'm fixing this situation. I'm not fixing it because I want something, I'm fixing it because I want to be better." Although it took some ups and downs, Lakesha continues to be just what she said she was going to be- a better mother, daughter, sister, friend, and overall person. When she told me that she was preparing to write a book to share her story, I knew then that the beaming process had started. I remembered those long brother and sister conversations that we would have about life and growth. Her story is just the beginning and the end is nowhere near! I pray that whomever reads this book, will know that to be healed from heartbreak, loss, and sadness, you must not be afraid to start the healing process.

Demetrius Hoyett

PREFACE

Here I am.
40 years old.
Divorced.
Raising two beautiful kids.

My two kids make me proud of them every day. My journey hasn't been easy. To be exact, far from easy. My trials have been far more difficult than I could have ever expected. You know, the last 8 years have been nothing more than a repetitive circle of events. It's been times of joy, sadness, bitterness, scares, and anger. But through all those good and bad times I learned a lot, got more spiritually connected, and found who I was as a person. God always protected me and my family throughout all my trials. Some of which I had no clue of what was going to happen to us next. Which brings me to "this" point in my life. I always knew I had a gift of helping others. I always had the tactic to help others see the good in themselves throughout a tough situation. Now, I have accepted that gift fully from God. I'm using my life's stories as testimony tools and my desire is that it gives others the encouragement they need to strive to see another day. The day my life took a complete turn was the day I had to search deep inside to dig up who I really was created to be...During this phase, I had to also find the strength to continue life. I remember the day my strength and my total existence (that I once knew) was taken away. It left me in complete loneliness. My marriage and family were the only thing that was of importance to me and to have that broken tore me to pieces! My marriage and kids were my pride and possession. There was nothing I wouldn't do to succeed for them...My family was the ultimate priceless possession that no one would have thought would end.

In this book I will share with you how I journeyed through many difficult situations. It's about how finding who I was created to be and how I discovered that developing a stronger relationship with my creator was the best thing ever! You will be exposed to some of my ultimate secrets, life lessons and some of the horrific challenges I faced through separation, divorce and single parent life. It was these valuable lessons that I must share so that they can help others. It was these lessons that made me who I am today. So many may ask the question, "What's so unique about her situation than anyone else's?", or "What makes her an expert in life situations?" Well, I asked God the same thing and this is the answer that He gave me (And now, I'm giving it to you). God told me that He took me through these trials so that I could be a blessing to others on so many levels. He said that He wanted to use what people view as an ordinary person and show them how extraordinary I am! God said that I want them to know how you went through your struggles and still stand to live and tell about it! He told me that He has given me a series of tests and that some I had to keep repeating, but finally, I passed. Because you are still standing, I'm using you to be a vessel to help others get to their happiness. I took you out of your comfort zone and built you up. I'm allowing you to share your life's testimony. Now, let's see how many lives we can change because of your obedience. YOU HAVE RECEIVED YOUR MASTER'S IN LIFE

LESSONS, now you are working on your PHD!!! Glory to God! So, this book is not only for the divorced. It has so much that can help anyone who's going through rocky life situations. It's for anyone who struggles with daily life situations that this world throws at you!

-Kesha

CHAPTER 1

Lord, tell me why my marriage had to end?

I got married back in 1997 and I was so very happy. See, it wasn't anything that I loved more than being married. I was young and thought I knew everything about the world. I thought that I would live a *happily ever after* type of married life. Of course, marriage wasn't always happy, but overall, I thought it was great. We were young so naturally things were a trial and error. I mean we were learning...Learning about finances and just simply understanding each other. We didn't really think about lifelong plans until years after we had been married. The only thing that was on the top of our list was having kids. Six months before we got married, we purchased a mobile home. We worked to the point that we thought we were making a lot of money and didn't put much consideration into saving any of it for the future. We pretty much lived for the moment. It wasn't until years later, after one kid and thinking about our future that we tried to do things differently in life. Shortly after, we had the opportunity to move to Florida due to employment for my husband. We were excited and anxious to go and start this new adventure. Things were ok the first year 18 months after moving; there were a lot of changes, but we dealt with it. I was busy with our daughter because she was doing some modeling with Disney. We also did a lot of exploring in the new area. Two years later, we were blessed with our son. Everything seemed great from what the outside world could see. But as fate would have it, things turned from better to worse quickly. I thought that my marriage was like any other marriage. It had its ups and downs, but again, I thought it was great. So, when it came to the hard times, I would work through the struggles. I wasn't a quitter and I didn't see myself quitting on the things I vowed to death do us part. I valued marriage to the fullest and was willing to work through any circumstances. I would always refer back to the scripture Matthew 19:6 (NKJV) *"So then, they are no longer two but one flesh. Therefore, what God has joined together, let no man separate."* The thought of getting a divorce was not an option in my book. Besides, who gets married and thinks that it would possibly end in a divorce? I married this man because I loved him. In my mind we were going to live happily and forever. But as you know, things aren't as we plan it to be sometimes. Proverbs 19: 21 (NIV) *"Many are the plans in a person's heart, but it is the Lord's purpose that prevails."* Sometimes, we don't understand why things happen, but as we keep living He will show you the plan. It wasn't in my plan to divorce my husband, but His plans are not my plans. The reason I left my ex-husband wasn't because of his infidelity. It was because he wasn't willing to change for his family and I wasn't willing to accept any more wrong doings. I tried to make things work and I did all I could to stay. I tried to talk, I pleaded, and I cried. But let me be the 100th person to tell you that when you ask God to reveal things, be prepared for what He shows you. Do not pray and then expect for things to always end up the way that you desire. I remember praying until the day I left. God revealed evidence to me that I thought I wasn't going to be able to handle. I remember getting on my knees and simply praying to God these words "If there is anything that needs to be revealed to me in this marriage that is not a part of you, please reveal it to me." He brought me directly to the light on issues that needed to be addressed. Let me tell you...I was praying that prayer, but was I truly ready for what was to come afterwards? Of course not, but I had to endure it because I asked God to show it to me. God wants you to come to Him for help, but don't get upset when the answer is revealed to you. There are demonic spirits in people that are assigned to destroy marriages. As you already know, the enemy does not care! The used vessels just get what they want and move on to the next target. I had been through this similar situation with my ex-husband before we got married. This time it was different and extremely difficult. I can admit this was the most trying times of my life. I was fighting for my husband with an outside woman. He told me on several accounts that he no longer wanted to be married. I still tried to stay after that, but it was like I was living with a stranger. It wasn't the same person I married. It was like someone had invaded his body. I couldn't continue to be disrespected and treated like I wasn't his wife and like I didn't mean anything to him. I had put too much into our marriage to have been disrespected. It was a series of events that led me to leaving and even then, I only left to make a stand. It was really supposed to be a temporary move. I thought that this would be a wakeup call and that he would come to reality. It didn't turn out the way I planned...In fact, the outside woman reached out to him more and made things worse. I'm not blaming her completely because he was the one married. On the other hand, I never dealt with someone who disrespected a marriage to the point of destruction. I had no clue that my marriage was in this much jeopardy. I couldn't understand why he would be so angry all the time and why I could never do anything right. But after everything revealed itself, it made sense why he couldn't concentrate at home. It didn't matter how hard I tried things just wasn't right before I left. I finally couldn't take anymore. I couldn't take any more fighting and fussing. I had to make a stand. I had to leave because it was so unhealthy, and I was afraid either he was going to hurt me or I would hurt him out of anger. Psalms 37:8 (ESV) *"Refrain from anger and forsake wrath! Fret not yourself; tends only to evil."* Sometimes you must know when enough is enough. You must know when your life or someone else's life is in danger and then come to a realization that it's not worth the trouble. It's best to walk away and cool down before you do something that you will forever regret.

Lord, I need clarity.

Like many people that have gotten a divorce, you begin to ask God a series of questions. Why did this happen to me? Was I the best person I could be in my marriage? Was there anything that I could have changed? Did he even love me? Those are just some of the things that go through your mind before you get to the angry and upset stage. I began asking God things like "Why did you give me the perfect family only for this to happen? How could you allow such pain to come into my life? Why would you allow me to be left alone raising two kids on my own? What did I do that was so bad that I'm getting punished?" I began saying things like "Surely my kids don't deserve this and neither did they ask for this. It's just not fair to us."

I was talking to God like I talked to an individual. I needed answers and He was the only one that could give it to me. I was faithful in my marriage and tried to live right. I needed Him to show me why He allowed me to go through such pain. I was so upset with God and my husband at the time. I just could not understand why my ex-husband was so evil towards me. I wondered at the time what did I do to him to be treated so bad. Heck, I felt like the woman had put some type of witchcraft on him. I had never seen him act in this manner and I just knew that she had done something to him...Maybe even brainwashed him in some type of way. Well, I had just about enough of the nonsense. I had gotten fed up of the crap that he was dishing out to me every day. Just because he was the *head of the house* didn't mean that I had to accept being treated like I was less than his wife...less than a woman. Don't get me wrong, he was a good father and a great provider, but that didn't give him the right to walk all over me. I just couldn't understand what was happening...he was no stranger to religion and he knew God. This man was a joy for everyone to be around. So, *I knew* that *he knew* right from wrong. He was a person that would go over and beyond for his family. It wasn't anything that he wouldn't do for us. Yes, he had issues just like anyone else and besides no one is perfect right? I don't want you to get confused... He wasn't a horrible person. Our marriage was admired by so many because we kept (what looked like) positivity going and tried to show love around others. We tried to be the family that would not be a stereotype. So, it was natural that I became confused when things began to take a left turn. Certainly, you can understand how I felt when he said, out of his mouth that he no longer wanted to be married...This was not what we prayed for and where did we go wrong? When did we lose our way? Some things we don't understand at the time, but we need to ask God for clarity. It's ok to ask God to show you clarity in *why* things happen. People say all the time we shouldn't question God. Look, if we don't ask Him for understanding of our situations, how are we going to grow through the trial? I think that He wants us to come to Him and ask questions. He wants us to grow and to be wiser through our trials. The only way to know an answer is to ask a question. You aren't asking Him to change His mind about your situation...You simply need His direction and need to know the directions to take. As I discovered, He is a perfect God and He already knows the plans for our future. You just need Him to show you how to be a strong warrior through the fight and how to come out victorious. It states throughout the bible to "ask". John 15:7 (KJV) *"If ye abide in me, and my words abide in you, ye shall ask what ye will, and it shall be done unto you."* and Luke 11:9 (NIV) "*So I say to you: Ask and it will be given to you; seek and you will find;*

knock and the door will be opened to you." I think that God loves the fact that we want to know why things happen in our lives. It is equally important to ask Him how your trial can help build up His kingdom. Always ask God to help you to see your situation with clarity. Psalms 119:130 (NIV) *"The unfolding of your words gives light; it gives understanding to the simple."*

Repetition Prayers: God, do you hear me?

I stayed in constant prayer over my family. I prayed over my kids and ex-husband every day. It wasn't a day that went by that I didn't pray and occasionally, we prayed together. Like any other person, I would pray harder when trouble was knocking at my door. You know, before I decided to leave my husband I prayed and asked God that if it was His will to restore my marriage. I tried so hard to stay before I made the decision to leave. Unfortunately, it didn't work out like that...I was tired of fighting and I just couldn't take it anymore. I literally felt drained, hurt, tired and misused. It seemed like the more I prayed the worst it got. I think we are programmed to talk and run to God in time of trouble and need. Then, when we go to Him, we want the answers and results quickly. We want the results to be what we want it to be. At this point I was praying more and more every day. I was praying the same prayer of restoration and if I was struggling with something else, I would make sure that it was included. As I think back, were my prayers really what they should have been? I mean was the prayer because of hurt just to make my marriage work? Well, the answer to that would be yes, but if you had asked me that years ago it would have been an easy no. Yep, I was praying, but I just wanted God to just fix it so that my marriage wouldn't end. I didn't care how it was mended I just wanted my marriage fixed. I spoke with God daily and I questioned myself. I mean was it more of just a repetition of words or prayers of sincerity? I think at times we tend to repeat the same prayers. God wants more of us than the same prayer every day. He already knows what we need before we ask Him. Often, we get so comfortable and feel we have to say things in a certain way and in a certain tone of voice just for Him to hear us. We can get so caught up in repetitive prayers that we begin to sound like a broken record. Matthew 6:7 (NIV) *"When you pray, don't babble on and on as people of other religions do. They think their prayers are answered merely by repeating their words again and again."* We only tend to take the liberty to pray harder or differently when trouble comes into our lives. We pray harder for others that go through their afflictions, not thinking that our storm will come one day. Sometimes, we tend to think that we are so set above the bar that we can't go through certain situations. I prayed to God every day, but I didn't pray deeply for my marriage because I had put my marriage inside an unbreakable box. I never thought this much trouble would arise that would cause a divorce. I prayed harder for financial situations than making sure that we were spiritually connected with one another. During that phase I thought that our finances were more important. It's only natural that you pray for things that affect you, yet we never really pray for the things that might come to pass. I guess I will call it a prayer of prevention. We fail to thank God for keeping our families together and for the blessings we already have in our possession. As I look back into my situation, I can say I had a lot of repetition praying. I didn't pray for God to touch him and change his heart. I didn't pray for God to help him see his own ways and to change them. I just continued to pray for my marriage to be restored if it was in His will. I didn't pray for our marriage to continue being healthy and strong daily. You know, it's safe to say that I was angry at him but was still in love...and perhaps I was a little bitter. I knew that he knew God so I just couldn't understand why he was doing those things. I couldn't understand why he chose this path of life. I thought he was the ultimate epitome of selfishness. It was only natural that I would feel this way. Let me tell you... If I had prayed the right prayers and not been so bitter and angry, maybe I probably could have gotten more clarity. There is no excuse for his actions and the things we went through. I'm not giving him a pass, but don't you love how God shows and gives confirmation on things that you prayed about? Even if it's years later... I was vulnerable and weak at that point in my life. I was tired of the bickering and fighting back and forth.

I thought I was way too good of a person to go through so much pain. If only I had prayed for God to show me clarity...If I had prayed for his strength... and what if I had of prayed about how to deal with this situation better? Things just might have been a little different. I'm not saying that I would have stayed in the situation, but I am saying that I would have been mentally, physically, and spiritually in a better position. I wasn't fighting the man I married, I was fighting an evil spirit within him. It was one spirit that still loved his family, but it was another one that was completely torn from his family. This spirit was connected to the evil of the world. I wasn't strong enough to fight with that evil spirit anymore. Sometimes, you can be torn down so much that you can't fight anymore. At that point either you can surrender your problems to God or take it into your own hands. I suggest letting God fight the battle for you. He will give you strength, encouragement, and wisdom to make it through. He must remove you from the situation to build you up so that He can mold you into the person that He created you to be. It just takes tough love. Public

Service Announcement: Those drive thru prayers that you give Him aren't good enough. God deserves a full discussion. He also wants you to ask for more. He will take you to a place where you can only depend on Him for help. He is the only one that will answer when there is no one else that understands. For this reason, He is making you stronger. And then, you can see His work. Haven't you noticed that it's at our lowest point that He gets our attention? Romans 8:28 (KJV) *"And we know that all things work together for good to them that love God, to them who are the called according to his purpose."* My ex-husband had been to war and lost his best friend, which was also his brother. I didn't realize that those things might have had a dramatic effect on his life. These events may have caused him to act a certain way towards us and other things may have also contributed to his disconnect. At that moment I only saw what was in front of me and what was in front of me wasn't the person I knew. It was a person I had never met- a person that I had grown to be afraid of because I didn't know the things that he was capable of doing to us.

All I knew is that I could no longer live in the same house with this man. This wasn't the same person that I made vows with. Even though I was weak, I was still stronger than he was. As a wife we should step in when our husband is weak and pray for him. I should have prayed for his strength and for God to bring him from the path of unrighteousness. We all know that the man is the head of the home and we fail to realize that they too can fall weak. As wives we were graced to be our husband's helpmate and intercede for him. I'm merely speaking on prayer life now. It doesn't matter rather or not if you or that person choose not to be together continue to pray prosperity over their life rather than sheltering anger. It can be hard to do this when you are angry, hurt and heart broken. But those things only create strong holds over your life. It's not about revenge. As I said before, it's about healthy relationships. It may be hard, but just taking that person by the hand and praying for them can break a chain of evil cycles that plague a relationship. And if you can't physically grab their hand, do it spiritually. I'm not saying stay in something that is clearly not meant for happiness, but what I am saying is to continue to pray for them as well as yourself. Romans 15:1 (KJV) *"We who are strong ought to bear with the weak and not to please ourselves."* I know some people wonder why we should pray and try to help our spouse when they're the ones who did wrong and the ones with the issues. True. They may have created the circumstances, but it is your problem as well. Remember since you are married you are now as one. Genesis 2:24 (KJV) *"Therefore shall a man leave his father and his mother and shall cleave unto his wife: and they shall be one flesh."* Husbands and wives are to help each other. I'm not saying just lay down and accept anything that they dish out...But most times you must go beneath the surface of the problem to see if there are other things that have triggered the issues being illustrated in the relationship. In some cases, it may be things that can be resolved. Some things can be fixed with a little more communication and more sincere talks with God. Remember, no drive thru prayers. Communication is a key element in making things work. Many fail to communicate by giving the silent treatment. When this is done, how do you expect anyone to know how you feel if you don't communicate. How do you expect them to help you if you never talk? Communicating effectively is always a plus. On the other hand, communicating when you are upset and fussing does not resolve the issue...It only magnifies it. If you don't have effective communication in your marriage, pray for it. Try taking your partner by the hand and praying together instead of praying separate. Both you and your spouse need to be on one accord in your household. Matthew 18:20 (KJV) *"For where two or three are gathered together in my name, there am I in the midst of them."* Just try this and watch how God manifests. It's imperative for husbands and wives to pray together. When we pray, we don't have to use all these big extravagant words to impress God. We just need to have a pure heart and a daily talk with Him...And let it not be so generic. If you are reading this and have a family, you need to come together and prayer as a family. Encourage everyone in your household to have their own prayer life with God. When you pray with your spouse and hear his prayers, you may find that there are things that he needs from God that you didn't know. Being in obedience to God and on one accord will ultimately position you for changes in your household that only God can make happen.

MY PRAYER

Dear God,

I come to you asking that you bring families closer together in prayer. Show them the powerful experience of when two or more come together in the name of Jesus. Let them know that you don't need a certain tone or a certain way to approach your throne. Let them know that you hear them in their distress and in their happiness. Let them know that everything in life must involve you. Father, I pray that they should always want to know more about you and want more of you in the family household to keep things in perspective. We know that the devil wants to destroy families with his evils, but you have the greatest power. Father my prayer for all homes is that they are blessed with a better prayer line to you. These blessings I pray in your son Jesus name,

Amen.

YOUR SCRIPTURE

Matthew 18:19 "Again I say unto you, that if two of you shall agree on earth as touching anything that they shall ask, it shall be done for them of my Father which is in heaven."

Psalm 107:28-30 "Then they cry unto the LORD in their trouble, and he bringeth them out of their distresses. He maketh the storm a calm, so that the waves thereof are still. Then are they glad because they be quiet; so, he bringeth them unto their desired haven."

John 14:13-14 "And whatsoever ye shall ask in my name, that will I do, that the Father may be glorified in the Son. If ye shall ask any thing in my name, I will do it."

Mark 11:24 "Therefore I say unto you, what things soever ye desire, when ye pray, believe that ye receive them, and ye shall have them."

What can I change in my life?

_____

_____

_____

_____

_____

_____

What are my goals to achieve it?

_____

_____

_____

_____

_____

_____

_____

CHAPTER 2

Living with your choices

The day that I made the hardest decision in my life to leave my ex-husband was a very painful day. On the day that I said it, it felt like I was issuing myself a death sentence. I can vividly remember the day I started packing the U-Haul truck. I knew it was going to be somewhat of a change for a while. As I was loading the truck, it felt like someone was stabbing a knife in my heart. I didn't want to leave, but at the time it was unhealthier if I had of stayed. I didn't want to leave the place that I called my home. I didn't want to leave my husband, the man that I loved and the father of my children. But we did more bickering than trying to fix things. It appeared that I was the only one that wanted this marriage. He was constantly telling me he wanted a divorce and his actions showed it as well. I moved back to Alabama and was literally devastated. I wasn't only leaving my husband, I also left my best friend. I was moving in the uncertainty of life. This is where I really had to trust God. Proverbs 3:5 (ESV) *"Trust in the Lord with all your heart, and do not lean on your own understanding."* Trying to understand life can be difficult. It is especially challenging when you are not close to God. You can't tell if you made a good or bad decision. You think that the path you have chosen is correct, yet still you are unsure. The first few months I left I definitely felt that way. In those moments I had to continue to trust that I made the right decision. In those moments I had to continue in prayer. I felt that this would blow over, but it didn't. I was in Alabama, but my mind and heart were still in Florida. I wasn't happy and it had started to affect me physically. When I moved back to Alabama with my mom, I thought it was temporary. It was challenging to move back home because I had been married for a very long time. I moved from having my own space to sharing a space. I had to adjust to having people around at all times and I know they had to adjust to us being there as well. I felt ashamed and embarrassed. There I was living with my mom with my two kids. No job and separated from my husband. I felt hopeless and angry. I felt like a failure and I didn't like that feeling at all. Being away from my home weighed on me mentally, spiritually, and physically every day. I began to lose a lot of weight. I lost around 50 pounds. It didn't matter how much I ate, I still lost weight. I had a pain in my back that I couldn't get rid of...It felt like I had razors in my lower back and I was always feeling fatigued. I was in and out the doctor's office with all kinds of testing. All the tests would come back negative or clear. Later I was diagnosed with depression and anxiety. I was prescribed medication that I chose not to take because I thought I could get better without it. I remember going to one of my doctor appointments and the doctor told me either you can take the medicine and get better or end up in the hospital. He looked me in the eyes and told me that he didn't think I realized how serious it had gotten. He told me that I have had some tremendous life changes and that it was ok to get help. He also told me that I wasn't the only one that had experienced depression or anxiety and that it was nothing to be embarrassed about. I learned that it's a chemical imbalance and that a lot of more people need to be treated. He told me that I needed to be strong and that I needed to get better so that I could raise my children. I started taking the medication to help with my anxiety and depression. Even though I wasn't the only one suffering from my diagnosis, I realized quickly that I had to be strong for the two little faces that depend on me. I took my medicine every day and started to feel better slowly. 1 Chronicles 16:11(KJV) *"Seek the LORD and his strength, seek his face continually."* I thought we would have been back in Florida, but the days just kept going by. I really believed that he would have come to get us and take us back home. I didn't really think that he would let his family go so easily. Eventually, the days turned into weeks and the weeks turned into months. I had to start looking for us a place to live. It was hard to believe, but after all of that, he still didn't want his marriage and wasn't trying for it either. It was hard for me because people would say things about what I should and shouldn't do. I didn't want to hear any of it. I knew it was only because they loved me and didn't want to see me hurting. But at the same time, I just needed space, a job and a place to live. I wanted to just run so far away from everything and not answer my phone or tell anyone where I was at. I was still hurting so of course I didn't want to hear the negative. I was already getting enough of that from my ex-husband. I didn't want everyone to know every detail of my broken marriage. I began searching for an apartment and it wasn't as easy to get one as I thought. Things just wasn't going as planned. It wasn't a lot of places to choose from and the places that were renting required me to go through a lot of red tape just to get approved. It took forever before I got an approval for a low-income apartment. I finally got the chance to move into my own place. I thought this would help me feel a little better, but I was so wrong.

JOB CHALLENGES

I moved into a low-income apartment and was happy to have my own space, but sad all at the same time. It was a two-bedroom, one bath. There wasn't anything fancy about it...It simply provided a roof over our heads. I literally would cry myself to sleep at night after I got my kids to sleep. This was definitely not what I had expected. I still didn't have a job, living in a low-income apartment and on food assistance. How could my life completely turn rapidly in a few months? The job search was limited and I tried some of everywhere. I finally found a job. I should have been grateful, but I think I was just going through the motions at the time. I knew I had to do something to provide for me and my kids. I also knew that I didn't want to live in that apartment forever either. The only downfall about the job was that I was on call and the pay wasn't great. If I got called in, I would have to get my kids up throughout the night and take them to my mom's house. Sometimes, it would be so cold outside and I had to get my 18 month old and my six-year-old up out of bed. I didn't have any other choice at the time other than being without money. I would get my check and would say this is only temporary. I knew in my heart that I wouldn't be working at that place for long, but my "temporary" turned into years. One day I got the bad news that the hospital was downsizing and guess who was in that reduction. Even though I didn't like the job I still felt like it was done unfairly. The people who were hired after me were able to keep their job. I didn't question the reason why I was chosen. I just took it and moved on. It was another life experience for me. I was hurt and angry at the same time. I was faced with the possibility that we might have to move again. I had to figure a way to tell my kids that I wasn't working. I continued to pray and ask God why things kept happening. I asked Him to please cover me and my children so we would not lose anything again. Joshua 1:9 (NIV) *"Have I not commanded you? Be strong and courageous. Do not be afraid; do not be discouraged, for the LORD your God will be with you wherever you go."* Throughout this transition from Florida to Alabama I had to remember that I prayed and that He had showed me things. I had to remember that I was the one that made the decision to no longer accept the way that I was being treated. I had to endure the process and trust what God was trying to show me. He didn't promise me that the process was going to be easy, but He did show me that I needed to remove myself during that time. All the things that I had to endure- the pain and hardship, it was necessary to prepare me for the person I am today. If I hadn't of went through that process I probably wouldn't have been able to have so many stories to help others. I wouldn't be sitting here writing a book to help anyone to succeed. When you find your purpose and learn that it is a purpose for everything it will help you deal with situations a little better.

MY PRAYER

Dear God,

We honor your name right now and I ask you to look over your people. Bless those who are discouraged because they have lost their employment. Bless them and let them know that not only will you give them something better, but that they will be able to bless others. Bless them with the joy of health and peace in their life. As they make decisions, bless them so that they do so with clarity. These blessings we ask in your son Jesus name,

Amen.

YOUR SCRIPTURE

John 16:33 "I have told you these things, so that in me you may have peace. In this world you will have trouble. But take heart! I have overcome the world."

Ephesians 1:17-18 "That the God of our Lord Jesus Christ, the Father of glory, may give unto you the spirit of wisdom and revelation in the knowledge of him: The eyes of your understanding being enlightened; that ye may know what is the hope of his calling, and what the riches of the glory of his inheritance in the saints."

What can I change in my life?

_____

_____

_____

_____

_____

_____

What are my goals to achieve it?

_____

_____

_____

_____

_____

_____

_____

CHAPTER 3

The Boomerang

Can you imagine having to move every year? Packing and unpacking furniture and clothes every year? Well, that was the story of my life. There were a lot of unanticipated moves. Just thinking about it is exhausting. Every year was like a roller coaster ride or an obstacle course. Some moves were made by choice and some weren't. Even though I had to move every year, I managed to find a roof over our head. We never went without the necessary things we needed. Throughout the moves I remained strong and learned to cope through those challenging situations. I told myself at least we weren't on the streets. I often said to myself, some people are in worst conditions. I had to adopt this type of mentality to make myself move forward. It felt like every year I was repeating the same issues. I would question God, "Why me?" I wanted to know why I had to move so much and go through so much in life. I started a pity party for myself and then I realized that it wasn't going to solve anything. I tried to do everything to the best of my knowledge. I would go to church and take my family as well. I would tell God that I know its people out there that deserve this type of treatment, but not me! I try to live right and take care of my kids, so why should I continue doing right and not get ahead? My first move was into a low-income apartment. It was a 2-bedroom apartment on the top floor. It didn't have a washer and dryer connection so I had to transport clothes back and forth to the laundry mat. It was a place that I would call home temporarily because I knew that I wasn't going to be there long. It was so depressing every time that I would enter this place. Ok. Let me give you a little background...I left a home that was worth over $200,000 and now I was living in low-income housing. Yes, it was a place of shelter, but such a total change! I would literally be depressed just pulling up in the parking lot. When I entered the apartment, I just wanted to cry, but I held all my tears until I was alone at night. After my kids went to sleep, as I said before, I would get in my own bed and cry myself to sleep. There were so many sleepless nights there. That apartment only held memories of pain for me. I worked so hard to move away from there so that I could get something better. I couldn't make this a final place for my kids to be raised. I knew what I wanted for them and this wasn't it. I searched and finally came across a house that I was able to rent which made my second move. It was a 2-bedroom, 1 bath home. This place was not the best, but better than the apartment. It was an older home and it needed work, but I was willing to fix on things. I thought this was a better decision. It had a backyard, but it needed new flooring. I purchased some stick tile to put in the bathroom and kitchen. I was trying to make it as comfortable as I could. I thought that this was an upgrade from where I was. Then one day I noticed the ceiling was getting lower and lower. I knew it was an older home but I didn't think that the ceiling would fall in! I had to end up packing up and moving again to another location. My third move was in a 3-bedroom, 2-bath duplex. It was much nicer than the last two I lived in. I was happier there because it was upgraded with appliances, flooring, and carpet. I didn't feel like a worthless parent when I brought my kids into this place. It had a fenced in backyard and they were able to play. I continued to work and strive for better. Then my landlord called me to tell me about another property that became available. It was even better than the place I was living in. I really thought God was answering my prayers. I don't know about you, but in my despair, I certainly thought He was passing me by... I felt as if I was on punishment. So, when this happened, I was excited. Psalms 86:1 (NIV) *"Hear me, Lord, and answer me, for I am poor and needy."* So of course, my 4th move was by choice. I moved to a 3-bedroom, 2- bath home. It was a newer home and everything was perfect. I really felt like I had finally accomplished something. I was happy to bring my kids home. It was a place I didn't feel bad about raising them. It was somewhere that I had a little peace. My kids had a place they could run around and play and not have to worry about neighbors. I enjoyed that place until the big news came that I lost my job. It was a strain to stay there because I couldn't afford to keep paying rent off unemployment. I couldn't find employment quickly either, so I had to move again. I really hated to tell my kids we were moving again. I knew they were tired of moving because I was. I was devastated and felt like a repeat failure. Why did these things keep happening to me? I felt like I was when I first moved into the first apartment. I found another low-income apartment, which brought me to my 5th move. It was better than the first low- income I lived in. It was a 3-bedroom, 2-bath. It wasn't that bad to live in considering the places I had previously been in. I still wasn't satisfied with where I was in life. I didn't want to continue this path of living in a low-income home. I continued my job search and it was unsecure in the area I was living in. I had to find employment an hour away. So, after driving back and forth for a while I decided that I needed to move closer to my job. The drive was mentally and physically exhausting. I started looking for a place to live closer. I decided that moving 20- minutes away from the job was better than driving an hour each way every day. I found a nice 3-bedroom / 2 -bath home in a nice community. I was excited to start this new journey. Yes, it was now our 6th move. It was something different, but a challenge. I wasn't close to any family so I had to trust that I would meet great people. This home was nice and had all the upgrades. We hardly were there because of work, school, and activities, but when we were, we enjoyed it. We stayed there a year before we got the news that we would have to move once again. The owner of the house decided that she wasn't going to use the real estate company that she had anymore. So, I had to move once again. The new real estate company didn't have anything in my budget at the time, so it forced me to search harder to find a place. I was beyond frustrated, tired, and hurt. See, just as soon as my kids would get used to something, then something would occur. I was at my wits end. This was becoming a repeated cycle that I hated and I knew people were tired of moving me every year. Eventually, I found a lady that was renting a home. She seemed to be a trustworthy and honest lady. I was happy because I had finally found a place within my budget and we didn't have to go back to living with family or not have a place to stay. The lady told me that she was moving out of state and was not looking to relocate back to Alabama. Well, everything seemed to be going great. I never saw her, but my neighbors would tell me that she lived with her mother. I told them that she was in Florida. Well, did I have a wakeup call...When I contacted her about renewing my lease she told me that she was moving back into the house. I was so upset because for an entire year I paid her mortgage while she got caught up on her bills. I was very frustrated. I wanted to punch every wall and throw every dish. I said I would never again rent a home from anyone else. I was stuck in a hard place. I wasn't prepared to move as far credit issues and money. I was turned down at some apartments and others said that I didn't make enough to live there. I didn't know where to go or what to do. I asked my aunt and uncle could we stay with them for a while until I was able to get somewhere for us to live. All I want to say is thank God for family. We at least had somewhere to stay until I could do better. At this point I was about to lose it. I just felt embarrassed and like a complete idiot. It seemed as if I was lugging and bouncing around everywhere. I literally wanted to put my kids in the car and keep driving until I couldn't drive any longer. I was tired of explaining myself every time we moved. This lead to our 8th move. I had to pack everything and put some things in storage. I was very grateful for them letting us live there, but I still felt like I was a burden. I was embarrassed because I never imagined that I would be without a place to live. I didn't think that my credit would be so destroyed that I couldn't get anything. There were times I really felt like giving up. I had to drive back and forth to work, drop the kids off at work, and stay for their extra activities. It was nights we would get home so late. I would be so tired and sleepy on the road. My kids would take naps in the car on the way home. I would look at them as they would sleep and say I have to do better. I had to keep pushing through the storms. I kept trying to look for somewhere to live while paying off some extra bills that I had. I got turned down for several apartments, but I finally got approved for another low-income apartment. I was excited because I was tired of driving and wanted my kids to have their space. I once again packed up and moved for the 9th time. This time I was happy, but I already knew that I wouldn't be living there long either. I estimated a couple of years give or take. It was just until I could get my credit on the right track. I was there a year before I had to go. I went to renew my lease and when my paperwork came back they told me that I was overqualified to live there. I was like here we go again. We are now going back through this same cycle. I was frustrated, but because I had gone through this process so many times I didn't worry as bad. I guess I was just fed up and tired. I didn't really look for a place until the last few weeks. I really began to speak with God. I knew that He wanted me to do something, but I wasn't sure if I knew how to do it. I heard God and I realized that I had a gift in me that He wanted me to share and maybe that's why I had to go through so much. It was at this point I just relaxed and let Him take over. It was a shift in my life. 1 Peter 5:7 *"Casting all your anxieties and worries on him because he cares for you."* I decided to let God lead my life. He spoke to me and I did what He asked me to do. God will allow you to move forward then bring you back to the same situation. I knew that it was something that I was missing. It was something that He wanted me to get that I didn't the first few times. He knew that sooner or later I would get tired and would submit to Him. He knows that we are hard hearted and stiff necked and that we want to do things our way instead of His way. He shows you until you do what is required, or you will have to repeat the process. I got tired of repeating the process and started to analyze my situation. I knew that this wasn't healthy for me. If only I could tune the world out and figure out what He needed for me to do so that I could succeed. God wants us to be successful and happy. Going through things is to make us strong, and to teach us valuable lessons. We must first figure out what He wants us to learn, then use that lesson to make our lives better and to help others. The key to success is to never give up and to never let your vision be blurred by the things you are going through. Talk to God and ask Him to show you the path that He wants you to travel. The path that He leads you on will someday help others. It's all about empowering yourself and others. I took a stroll to see what I was missing. I started letting him in and not just a little, but over my entire life. I wanted Him to make Himself known to me and to make the vision that He had for me clear. I really needed my never-ending cycle of going nowhere to end and I needed it to end fast. In time I was able to help myself and in return help someone else. I told Him that whatever He needed me to do that I was willing to do it because I was truly tired of feeling defeated. God said to me that He had been showing me what I needed to do, but instead of listening to Him I was listening to my own thoughts. It's easier sometimes to trust your own thoughts than to trust the vision that God has shown you. The vision that He has shown you will seem hard and impossible. God wants more of you. Let Him use you. Step out of your comfort zone and hold on tight to faith. Remember, you only need that grain of a mustard seed. However, you must put in the work and make the vision happen. When He shows you the assignment or the vision you must execute it to its fullest potential!

MY PRAYER

Dear God,

Thank you for allowing certain situations to come into my life. I don't understand them all the time, but I want to thank you for showing me clarity. Always show me my purpose in allowing me to repeat things that I should have gotten already. Give me the strength, comfort, and understanding to do what is needed to help myself and others. Let me be that shiny jewel that stands out from the others. The jewel that magnifies and helps others to be successful and happy! Let them see that the repeat events are only tests that they have failed. Show them what they need to pass it. Also, give them the courage to help others because this life is not about being unhappy, it's about being successful and happy to help others to be successful. These blessings I pray in your son Jesus name,

Amen.

YOUR SCRIPTURE

Psalm 119:18 "Open my eyes, that I may behold wonderful things from your law."

Psalm 119:165 "Great peace have those who love your law, and nothing can make them stumble."

What can I change in my life?

_____

_____

_____

_____

_____

_____

_____

What are my goals to achieve it?

_____

_____

_____

_____

_____

_____

_____

_____

CHAPTER 4

Falling for The Representative...

Have you ever had times in your life where you questioned the mindset of the person you were talking to? I mean really, have you ever thought to yourself this person has a lot of personalities, so whom I'm speaking with today? Do you ever wonder if anyone cares about other people's feelings? Some people may not have had those thoughts, but I have. These types of thoughts come from being with someone that have misled you. It makes you feel like some people are telling you something to benefit you or just plain out liars! It's the people that are closest to your heart that causes the most pain. I'm going to take you back to a place that I was totally fooled by the representative. At this point I had been separated for about a 18-months. I was living in the duplex apartment and things were going well. As you recall before I had been in some horrible living situations before I moved into this place. I was still in love and hurt, but I was moving on. I worked and took care of my kids and tried to stay busy as much as possible. Well, my ex-husband had a family member that died so we were in contact with each other before he left Florida to come back for the funeral. In one of the conversations I had with him, he expressed how he was sorry and wanted his family back. I was shocked and surprised because this was out of nowhere. Of course, I was happy and excited and couldn't wait to see him because it seemed too good to be true. I was overjoyed and couldn't wait to see my husband. He arrived and things seemed to be going as planned. He apologized and explained to the kids his mistake and that we were moving back. It seemed like everything that I prayed for was taking place. He even talked to my family and told them how he missed us and that he wanted us back. The kids and I were so happy. I couldn't tell you how much I was ready to go back home. It was a long time coming. We had decided to wait until December to move because of the transition of school for the kids. It would be over the holidays. This is what I had been praying for all these years and now it seemed to be coming true. It felt unbelievable and I tried to not think of the possibility that something bad could happen. He returned to Florida and things seemed to be going well. We talked every day about our plans. It seemed to be going great until one day I didn't hear from him. He didn't return any of my calls or my texts. I thought something had happened. The next day I called him at work and I noticed a change in the tone of his voice. When he got off work he called me back and I was shocked to hear what he had told me. Once again, he tells me that he doesn't want to be married anymore. At first, I held on to the phone with tears in my eyes...Then I asked him if he was serious and how could he do this to us again. I asked myself how did I fall for the lies once again? The person that I had been talking to before, where was he? I felt like someone had ripped my partially healed heart apart. It was like reliving a nightmare. I felt like we were used to be a display at family functions...Just a showcase. Our feelings weren't taken into consideration. It was a one man show and he was calling the shots. The day he told me this was on a Sunday. It was raining. I was so upset that I put my kids in the car and was headed to Florida. I was on my way to tell him just what I thought about him. I was fed up with the treatment and I was angry that I had allowed this to happen to us again. I was headed down the road crying and hitting the steering wheel. I was so upset that I had to pull over and get myself together because I couldn't drive any more. I looked back at those two faces and decided it wasn't in the best interest for me to take the kids on that long trip while being upset. I turned around and went back home and just laid in bed all day. How could he come and disrupt the life that we were rebuilding? When we spoke again, I told him he should explain to our kids that they weren't coming home. It was the only fair thing to do, but he told me that he wasn't going to and that I needed to just go on like things were before. I was left telling my kids that we weren't moving back home and with answering all the questions. My life was back to a point where I didn't want to be and it was physically and mentally wearing me down. I was over this thing called life. I just didn't think I was going to ever be happy. I started thinking that I was cursed. The only thing that kept me going was my kids. They were the ones that depended on me every day to be strong even when I didn't want to be. Like me, you must realize that things happen in life. Those things might be good and some bad, but it happens for a reason. Some things happen that we don't understand to protect us from future hurt and pain and to protect us from things that we don't deserve. We go through things that are difficult and we don't know the reasoning. But as time passes it is revealed to us. We are protected throughout our hurt and we don't realize it because we are going through the storm. We think that God has left us, but He hasn't. He really is protecting us because He knows our hearts and what our future will be. He knows what He has for us, but we can't even imagine it. We must be willing to go through the storm to reap the blessing and rewards at the end. I had to pull myself from this pit of sorrow and grief once again and fast. I couldn't allow this to take over my life. I had to keep fighting another day, even though I wanted to give up...I couldn't allow that to happen.

MY PRAYER

Dear God,

Thank you for revealing what a person truly feels about us. It might not feel good at times, but I know it's working for a greater cause in my life. In time I know that the purpose will be evident, but until then just continue to comfort me in my time of hurt. Thank you for your protection from future hurt of the things that will try to enter my life. Continue to provide a shield around me. Show me my purpose and let me have more strength than ever before. These and all other blessings I ask in your son Jesus name,

Amen

YOUR SCRIPTURE

1 Peter 3:9 "Do not repay evil with evil or insult with insult. On the contrary, repay evil with blessing, because to this you were called so that you may inherit a blessing."

Romans 12:21 "Do not be overcome by evil but overcome evil with good."

What can I change in my life?

_____
_____
_____
_____
_____
_____

What are my goals to achieve it?

_____
_____
_____
_____
_____
_____
_____

CHAPTER 5

Lord, tell me why love hurts...

There is a huge difference in being in love with someone and just loving them. When you're in love with that person you can't see yourself without them. You do whatever it takes to make sure you show them they mean the world to you. It's a feeling like no other to be in love. Most people don't think about it like this but being in love doesn't necessarily mean you're in love with your spouse. Example: You can be in love with your kids. The difference of course is obviously the intimacy; But the common denominator is that you would go through great lengths to make sure that your family is protected. You do not want to see them hurting for anything and you will support them. They hold a very important key to your heart that no one else can get to besides God. So, when they do something that is not favorable to you it hurts a lot more than if someone else did it. It's a pain that only they can give you if they did something wrong to you. The hurt and pain lasts for a long time. It doesn't just go away quickly and sometimes the pain causes a major effect on your life. When you are in love with a person you will accept a lot of things that you wouldn't tolerate with anyone else. We have more patience with them. We learn to adapt to their ways even if some things irk you. You will sometimes sacrifice things for yourself to make sure they are happy. It's well worth the sacrifice that you made just to see them happy. Most people will lay down their life to protect their kids. That's the same thing that Jesus did for us. So, can you imagine how Jesus feels when we betray and hurt him? Probably the same way, we feel when our spouse or children hurt or betray us. It's a feeling that only they can cause and only God can heal over time.

KIDS NOTICE

Like most parents, your kids are your world. They are your seed and an image of you. They are the blessing that God granted you and it's only natural that if they hurt, you hurt. That's natural for a parent, right? It's natural to want the best for your family. You would protect them from all hurt, harm, and danger. You would try to shield them from the everyday troubles of the world if you could, but instead you prepare them for the everyday world knowing that one day they will be leaving home and have their own family. Let's take a stroll back into my life situations. I did a self-evaluation of a time frame before moving out from my ex-husband. It was a time frame with a 6-month period and what I found wasn't pleasing. My ex-husband and I did a lot of arguing and it wasn't healthy for the kids to see. We did not show a lot of happy emotions around them like we used to and the words that we used weren't healthy for us to say or for our kids to hear. As parents, we must realize that we might get upset, but we should try not to show those angry emotions in front of our children. It's best to wait and discuss issues when the kids are not around. I know..it sounds easy right? When you are in the moment you are just trying to get your point across and you really don't think about who's around. But realize that the kids take it all in and it sometimes have such a negative impact that it might affect them in an unhealthy way. It might eventually cause an effect on their physical well-being. It may also affect them in the way they interact with others. One simple word or action might change your children's life and you didn't even know it. As a matter of fact, when you think about it, is the argument with your spouse in front of your kids really worth the emotional effect it may have on them? No, of course not. We all dream of having the perfect life, the perfect kids, and the perfect house. But guess what- things happen and we are dealt situations that we don't want to face. It's up to us to make the best out of a bad situation. It's up to us to try and pull our way out and do better for ourselves. If we don't the devil will just have a field day with our thoughts and actions. Our actions can be altered if we don't have a positive influence in our life. That could be simply reading a good spiritual book, listening to motivational music, or simply reading the bible. It's so easy to engage in a bad situation and say things that you shouldn't if you don't have a positive atmosphere.

1 Corinthians 15:33 *"Do not be deceived: Bad company corrupts good morals."* I always try to be careful on what I let my children see or hear especially when I might have a dispute with someone. If I have experienced emotional effects from the things that I have seen and heard, I know that my children will have an emotional effect from the things that I have allowed them to see and hear. A lot of what we do can be controlled. We are the adults and not the children and they shouldn't see us acting out. Try to engage in more conversation with your children to see how they feel about things. Let your kids know that they aren't the reason for the problem and both parents love them. It doesn't matter what kind of situation that you are in with your past relationships it shouldn't affect the way you love your kids. As parents, we must learn to cope with our differences and show unity in front of them. If you don't talk with your kids they may begin resorting to

different things to show their frustration or anger. Some kids don't know how to accept the changes that you as parents decide to make. It's up to us to make it as smooth as possible. Just think about it...the kids don't have a choice in the matter. They are stuck with whatever decision that you decide to make. I'm not saying that your decision is right or wrong. What I'm telling you is that children go through things and suffer from the same situations as adults. Their lives change as well. I thought that my daughter was coping well with the situation. I knew she missed her dad and wanted to go to his home sometimes. During that transition, she was a strong little girl. She was a happy child and I tried my best to make things comfortable for her and my son. I didn't let her see me cry, but truth is I cried plenty of nights. I kept her involved in activities, so I really thought things were ok with her. It wasn't until one day I was getting her ready for school and she had a complete meltdown. She clinged to me and cried for dear life. She wouldn't let me go and she thought something bad was going to happen to our family. It didn't matter what I tried to do I could not console her. I had to rush her to the doctor because I didn't know what was wrong with her. I found out she was suffering from anxiety. I did not see the signs. I overlooked the obvious. Every time I took her for a checkup the physician would ask how she was doing, how was she adapting to the move. My response was always she was doing good...at least I thought. The doctor told me that my daughter was use to her mother and father in the same household and that separation affects some kids totally different than others. Sometimes, it only takes a little something to trigger the anxiety after such a drastic change. I felt like a terrible parent because how could I not know that she was suffering. That was a major blow for me. I had to learn how to cope with the anxiety and stress of my daughter meanwhile managing my own anxiety and depression.

I learned to listen and watch for things more closely. Things that I thought wasn't a big deal meant a great deal to my child. Your child has feelings and sometimes they will not talk to you about it in fear of what the outcome might be, so just let them know that regardless of whatever happens, that they can always come to you. Let them know that as a parent and child you can work through any issues together and they are not alone. Let them know that it is ok to speak to someone that they trust if they don't want to speak or confide in you. Being open with your kids when you are going through a tough situation will help not only your child, but you as well. It will help them understand that they are not the cause and that both parents still love them the same. Do not let your child try to figure this out on their own. Don't be so selfish that you put your own regards and feelings before theirs. It's not their fault and they shouldn't be put in the midst of the situation to be made to feel as though they are. Most children know more than what you think they do. They not only watch both parents, but they have a determining factor about how they feel about how their parents are acting. As a result, I know that it's easy for you to be caught up at being angry at your spouse. Some parents use their kids as bait to get the other one to act a certain way. They don't want the kids to interact with the other parent only because they are upset. Meanwhile, your kids suffer. Your kids now see you as acting like the child. They don't understand why it's so hard for you two adults to get along especially when you preach to them to get along with each other and others. And, they don't understand why one parent is talking bad about the other parent. In their eyes you are still their parents. They are kids and that's exactly what their role should be. We shouldn't put them in any position to be anything other than that. Just know that kids remember and as they grow older they will develop their own opinions and you don't want to be the reason that your child grows up bitter. I say to you that if you can co-parent to make things better for your kids that's a great way to go. Show unity in front of them and let them know that despite anything that is going on, they are the main concern and you as parents will make sure that they are always loved. At this point when it comes to the children it's not about your own wellbeing it's about what's best for the child. If that parent is a good father or mother then the child shouldn't be kept from the parent. Let's promote healthier relationships when it comes to the kids. Besides, we are raising them to conquer this world and there's enough stress without us as parents adding to the plate!

MY PRAYER

Dear God,

We want to thank you in advance for the knowledge and wisdom you show us to conquer situations. Bless our children to be strong and able to handle things that are beyond their control. But show us as parents when to speak certain things around our kids and to think of our kids when we are making certain decisions. Give us the strength as parents to come as one to help our kids understand that we love them. We speak peace over our children lives and declare that they are not suffering from anything that they can't tell us as parents. We know that you have the power to make all situations that look bad turn into something awesome. This prayer we ask of you in your son Jesus name we pray,

Amen.

YOUR SCRIPTURE

Colossians 3:14 "Above all, be loving. This ties everything together perfectly."

Corinthians 16:14 "Let all that you do be done in love."

What can I change in my life?

_____
_____
_____
_____
_____
_____

What are my goals to achieve it?

_____
_____
_____
_____
_____
_____
_____

CHAPTER 6

Single Life Is Not for Me...

Okay, so now I'm divorced and back on the dating scene. Can you imagine how hard this was for me after being with someone over 16 years? Just imagine being in jail and life outside of prison is still going on and you only know what you're use to in prison. I'm not referring to my marriage as a prison, but I'm merely making a comparison. I mean you haven't been with another person in so long that the dating scene has changed and you haven't even noticed because you didn't need a date. It would be the same as letting someone out of prison and expecting them to adapt to the outside world and they have been incarcerated for so long. If you are in tune with the things in your home you will not be distracted by the outside influences. So, when it was time for me to date, I felt so out of place. I wasn't comfortable. It seemed that the choices that I had to pick in men were worse. It was only 16 years later what did I expect. I thought it was going to be very quick for me. I didn't think it would take me long to find someone and fall back in love and be married again. But I was so wrong. After going out and seeing what the world had to offer it wasn't all that great. I came to the assumption that maybe I needed to be a little more patient. Maybe I was trying to rush something and that's why I couldn't find that right one. I would go out sometimes when I got a chance and the men were far from flattering. I'm not saying all men was like that but the ones I met wasn't what I was looking for. I was going through these phases and to these places in hopes of meeting prince charming. I did meet some guys that I would immediately fall for and would hit it off with, but it never happened. All I would end up with was a friendly conversation for that night and good laughs with friends. And the other guys that would have any potential would already be married, in a relationship, or either not looking for anybody. After never meeting anyone I began to think that it would never happen. Then I decided I would just stop looking for someone and just focus all my energy on my kids. Besides, if it's meant to be, it will happen. I got introduced to someone and he was the sweetest guy. We dated for a couple of months. Then he got the news that his transfer went through and would be moving to Texas. I was hurt because for the first time I thought maybe I could finally be happy. We weren't at the point where we were thinking about relocating or a long-distance relationship. The relationship ended as soon as it started. I was hurt because I finally met someone that I could relate to and we shared some of the same common grounds and chemistry. Then it was another year before I met someone again that I found interest in like that. I met him at the post office. The funny story about that was that I had prayed all morning to meet someone because I was lonely and ready for someone to be in my life for me and my kids. So of course, when I bumped into him I thought my prayers were being answered. But much like the person before, he got orders to move to Texas as soon as we started talking good. I did gain a great friend out of it, but I was totally hurt. I cried and asked God why does he keep letting me meet people then take them away. I was so confused about what was going on. Am I such a bad person? I don't deserve to be happy? What have I done that I can't be happy? Afterwards, I met a man that wanted to rush into the relationship and get married after talking to me on the phone for a week. He got me a ring after taking me on two dates. But I wasn't use to that kind of fast action. He didn't know anything about me as well as I didn't know much about him so how could he want to marry me quickly. I just wanted to be like a normal person date and allow things to develop naturally without any pressure, but things just weren't working in my favor. Then, it was another guy...a great guy, but he aggravated me more than I enjoyed being around him. Being friends was better for us. I knew that my standards were simply on another level and I was so strong on security that I probably pushed a few good men who were actually trying away. I had my struggles to work through, but I felt like I couldn't bear any extra weight. This new way of dating was taking a toll on me. The guys that were truly and genuinely interested - I had no interest in them. That's when I found myself doing a self-evaluation again. I was convinced that God was showing me that there were good men out there, but he wasn't ready for me to meet them yet. He knew that I wouldn't complete His task first and knew that I would have been more focused on making them happy than finding myself. I look back and understand why those things happened. I understand why He removed those two that I cared so deeply for far from my presence. It wasn't because He was hurting me, He was preparing me for my greater. I don't know who God has for me, but just knowing who I am now makes it better for the next person who enters my life. I no longer have to suppress what God has birthed out of me and I don't have to live my life the way someone else wants me too. The next person will accept me for who I am and will love me for what I am.

MY PRAYER

Dear God,

Thank you for my disappointments in relationships. It has shown me who I am and what I am capable of. Through this process you have shown me gifts and talents that I have that have been buried. I'm thanking you in advance for preparing me for the husband that you choose for me. Let him be the man that you sent and designed especially for me. Let him love me for my perfections and imperfections as I would love him. Everyone that is going through a time of failing relationships, show them why it's failing and show them how it can be mended or used for growth. These blessings we pray to you in your son Jesus name,

Amen.

YOUR SCRIPTURE

Philippians 4:6-7 "Do not be anxious about anything, but in everything by prayer and supplication with thanksgiving let your requests be made known to God. And the peace of God which surpasses all understanding, will guard your hearts and mind your minds in Christ Jesus."

Romans 12:12 "Be joyful in Hope, patient in affliction, faithful in prayer."

What can I change in my life?

_____
_____
_____
_____
_____
_____

What are my goals to achieve it?

_____
_____
_____
_____
_____
_____
_____

CHAPTER 7

Drowning in debt...

Being by yourself and raising two kids is not an easy task. It's not one that I wish on anyone. In the past years I have been living from check to check. I had my cars repossessed. I have filed bankruptcy. I have had to go without plenty of days so that my kids could have the extra that they needed. I had to get food assistance at one point. Those things I'm not proud of, but they made me who I am today. I am not ashamed to say that I had to borrow money and sometimes didn't know where I would get gas to make it to the next week. People would probably think I was living above my means but I was only trying to survive. When I first moved back to Alabama I didn't have employment and had to apply for food assistance...plus I wasn't working and that's how I qualified for the low-income apartments. That was a terrible way to live. I didn't want my children to be raised there and I wanted to work and provide a decent life for them. I wanted to be able to have them in extra-curricular activities. I was making ends meet and sometimes I had a few dollars to hold me over to the next pay period. I had a wreck after I moved. The truck that I had that was paid for was no longer in good shape. It was in and out of repair and I had to put the title up for collateral at one of the money stores just to continue to pay bills and make sure that I had a ride back and forth to work. In between time I was accumulating medical expenses that I couldn't afford to pay. The truck kept giving me fits so I let it go. I knew that I had it on the type of loan that wouldn't report it to my credit so I just let them have it. I went to a dealership and purchased another car that I thought was dependable. Now, I had a car payment added with the other bills. Fortunately, I had family that would buy groceries and that would help me save money. I was managing, but barely. I did this for a while until it became the norm. I was making $12.00 an hour and was considered overqualified for a low-income apartment.

If you get any ounce of child support they include it as extra income and all your money is going to rent, daycare, utilities and after you subtract it you have nothing. The people that try so hard to be better are the ones that struggle with help. I wasn't going to be in that position for long so if I had to work overtime then I just had to do it so that my kids had what they needed. We managed that for a long time and things were going ok. It wasn't easy at all, as a matter of fact, it was far from it. My kid's happiness was the only thing that brought happiness to me. To see that they were comfortable and happy made me feel better. It gave me a purpose for the struggle. I knew that when they looked at me they didn't see anything but mommy providing. They didn't see the hurt and the pain from my struggles. There were a lot of times that I had to pawn my laptop until I got paid just to pay my utilities. It was a lot of times I was in and out of those check cashing places. I finally had to file Chapter 13. I look back and give all the praise and glory to God for helping me overcome that situation. He brought me out of that bondage. There were times that I thought how in the world am I going to make it... But God was always there for us. The day I got laid off from my job I ended up having to move back into a low-income apartment. I was upset because I lost what I worked so hard to keep. I was left depending on assistance once again and I was angry. I was angry about a lot of things like having to continue making payments on the bankruptcy that had shot my credit up. I couldn't afford anything extra on my plate. I spoke with an attorney about my options for my bills...I was already in a Chapter 13 and trying to convert to a Chapter 7. Starting over was the best option for me and this option included letting my car go back. It would also include me getting another car. So that's exactly what I did...got another vehicle. I was trying to start over and it was working out well. I found a new place to live and moved there yet still living from check to check, but I was good. I had medical expenses that came up again and because I didn't have the extra to pay, it also affected my credit. My score started going down again. If I paid on the medical bills it would make my car payment behind. It was just a trending cycle. There were extra things that my kids needed for school and of course that came first. It was a one income home...And believe me, there wasn't any extra assistance once I started back working full-time. I needed a job that paid at least $20 an hour. I wasn't making that and I was nowhere near it. I stayed in prayer and was able to work overtime hours to pay my bills. As I look back, I truly don't know how I could have accomplished the things I've done without God. He has shown me over and over that He will take care of me. I know that the vision that He showed me is much greater than me...And more importantly, I need Him to accomplish it. He took me through this period to understand that my brokenness is not about me. He wants me to have all that is promised to me and all that He has shown me in a vision. He also wants me to obey Him. I was at a place where I was afraid to obey Him. I was scared that I was going to fail the mission. He showed me that if you do what I ask I will supply you with more than enough. It was only when I went to a Women's

Conference that this was reassured to me-That God doesn't want me to be afraid. He wants me to be bold and courageous. He wants me to speak greatness to His people. He wants me to share my story. He showed me that if you do these things I will reward you. Romans 2:6 *"God will repay each person according to what they have done."* As you read in His Word He promises to repay you for the work you have done. So, you must do the work! Sometimes, doing the work might be when you have to go through your brokenness...but just know your reward will be plenty!

MY PRAYER

Dear God,

Thank you for when it seemed like I didn't have anything, you showed me I had something. Even when I didn't have enough you provided for us...we went through all those trials and tribulations and I never went without a meal or shelter. Continue to bless me with abundance overflowing so that I can help someone else. Let me be able to show someone else how to bless others. Let your people know that they are not alone and that you will not leave them. Let them know that the things that we go through is to make us stronger. Continue to bless us physically, mentally, and financially. These blessings I pray in your son Jesus name,

Amen.

YOUR SCRIPTURES

James 1:12 "Blessed is the one who perseveres under trial because, having stood the test, that person will receive the crown of life that the Lord has promised to those who love him.

1 Peter 5:6 "Humble yourselves, therefore, under God's mighty hand, that he may lift you up in due time.

Romans 2:6 "God will repay each person according to what they have done."

What can I change in my life?

_____

_____

_____

_____

_____

_____

What are my goals to achieve it?

_____

_____

_____

_____

_____

_____

_____

Chapter 8

Someone prayed for me...

It was a few years ago when I got the scare of my life. My son had a cyst on the back of his head that I had been keeping a close watch on for a few months. I was told by my doctor that if it didn't shrink that he would refer me to a specialist. A few weeks passed and it didn't shrink, so we saw another doctor. We went to see the specialist and he suggested a small outpatient surgery where he just removes the cyst. It seemed clear and easy, but it went from something simple to a trial and test. We arrived to get the cyst removed that morning. Everything was going as planned until the doctor came in the room to give me the results of the procedure. He came into the room and I wasn't expecting anything other than great news.

Remember, this was only a cyst nothing more so it should be simple. He looked at me and said he was recovering great, but what he had found was a little disturbing. I sat up in the chair with tears in my eyes and asked him what he meant. He told me I don't know what this is and that he hasn't seen anything like it before and that it was growing across his brain. He said that he had taken out what he could and sent it off for biopsy. He told me that he was referring my son to children's hospital. I immediately started crying and my heart sank. Things turned so quickly. I really don't remember anything else after he said that. I only remembered my mom saying to me "Kesha you have to pull yourself together and be strong for him because he doesn't understand. If he sees you upset then he will be upset." I know it was tough for her also because I could see it all over her face, but she stood strong. I dried my face up and went into the recovery room with my son. I can remember him holding his arms out for me. I held him tight and said a silent prayer with tears streaming, but I was so careful not to let him see. It was a week later before we saw the specialist and it seemed like the longest week ever. I was on edge and couldn't sleep nor concentrate. I was becoming angrier at God because I wanted to know why He kept picking on me! I understand choosing me to go through things, but do you really have to use my child? I told him they are young and innocent. Why would you choose my kids that are so precious and adorable haven't they been through enough? Their parents have just been divorced and all these transitional moves. I'm tired and I really don't think it's fair. I would go from being angry at Him at times to praying to Him and asking Him to heal my child. My faith was so shaken. I had a lot of people and family that prayed for me. I had a lot of people that talked to me and gave me good spiritual advice. I was shaken up and often asked the question what's the purpose for trying to be a good spiritual person? I thank God that He placed powerful spiritual people around me that prayed for me at this time. They stood in the gap of my brokenness. When I was tired and questioned my faith, their continuous prayers were still going to God. That's why it's good to be connected to the right people.

People that are connected to God. If the ones you're connected to can't pray for you when you need them to pray or can't give you good sound advice when you're in need, then you really don't need them...it's time to disconnect yourself. You don't need people when you are always feeling happy you also need people when you're down and out and feeling bad. The day we went to see the specialist I was nervous. Even though I prayed I was still thinking the worst. We arrived at the office and while I was sitting and waiting on the doctor to come in, I was still praying. The doctor came in and introduced herself. She began to explain to me what she thought it was. She sent us to do another test and we went back to the office. I was so shocked to get the best results ever. The doctor said that this was just a simple cyst and that it had burst on the inside and began to spread. The best results were that the tissue they sent out was not cancerous and the cyst drainage dissolved on its own. I was so happy and relieved that was something so simple. The situation looked bad, but when God intervened, He turned it into something good. My son was healed and healthy and the stress of worrying was relieved. God wants us to depend on Him and believe that He will work things out. That's why we depend on God because He can do the impossible things. These are Supernatural powers only you know that God can provide. Psalms 56:3 *"When I am afraid, I put my trust in you."*

MY PRAYER

Dear God,

Thank you for allowing the bad to turn into good. Thank you for sending people my way that are connected to you. Thank you for allowing them to pray for me in my time of need. The time that I didn't have the strength to pray and the strength to be connected to you they intervened. Thank you for allowing me to see that all things that look bad really aren't. Just because I realize this, I hope someone else will. God touch and heal the people that are going through a medical condition. Let them know that you have not left them. Also, send your angels to their needs. Send people to comfort them that are connected to you. And as they go through this journey, let them learn from this experience. We pray all these blessings in your son Jesus name,

Amen.

YOUR SCRIPTURE

PROVERBS 3:5- 6 "Trust in the Lord with all your heart and not on your own understanding; in all your ways submit to him, and he will make your path straight."

PSALM 56:3 "When I am afraid, I put my trust in you."

What can I change in my life?

_____

_____

_____

_____

_____

_____

What are my goals to achieve it?

_____

_____

_____

_____

_____

_____

_____

CHAPTER 9

Repossession?

I know you probably think that this chapter is about someone leaving me, but this chapter is far from that. This is more about what my challenges were during the time when my car was repossessed. I had learned through this phase how to be humble, patient, and how to let go of my pride. I had a car and it had started giving me trouble. For an entire year it was in and out of the mechanic shop for something, plus I had to get it towed on several occasions. I had money saved but exhausted it trying to keep the car working. It came to the point where I got behind on my car payments trying to keep the car going. I tried to keep the bills going but once you get behind and are the only source of income, it's hard to catch up. The car was causing me so much trouble and stress. But I knew I needed transportation so I kept trying to make things work. I had to make payments on mechanic work at times which added another bill in the household. The day that my car was repossessed was devastating. I had just made a payment and spoke with a representative about payment arrangements but when I woke up that morning to go to work it was gone. I was heartbroken and tired. My daughter turned and looked at me and asked me where our car was...I had to quickly get them on the bus because the next one was coming around the corner. I told her I would explain to her later. After they got on the bus I laid across the bed and just cried. I was so hurt and angry. I tried so hard but still ended up losing. I called my mom and told her and the first thing she said was it's going to be ok. We will figure it out and you will be ok. I just cried and told her that I was so tired. and that I don't know why I try. She told me that God sees me...He knows that I will be ok and that I can't give up because I have two kids depending on me. The next phone calls I made were to my brothers. I felt bad telling them what happened. I felt like I was a complete failure. They didn't judge me all they said was it would get better. By the end of the day I went from having no car to having two cars. Do you know that God will provide for you? I didn't go overnight without having any transportation. If you have trust that God will provide then it shouldn't be any worries. Philippians 4:19 *"And my God will supply every need of yours according to his riches in glory in Christ Jesus."* 2 Corinthians 5:7 *"For we live by faith, not by sight."* The hardest thing was to explain to my kids that we lost our vehicle. When they got home I explained to them that we no longer had the car. I tried to tell them in a way that they wouldn't be worried about me or things that was going on...besides, your kids shouldn't have to worry about things like that. As adults we try to shelter our kids from the hurt in the world. The last thing I wanted for them was to be burdened with adult issues. I simply put it in a way that the car was causing too many problems and in and out of the shop so mommy had to get another one. As I told them, they still proceeded to ask questions. They were more worried about me and if I was ok. I tried to hold back tears telling them that mommy would be ok. I told them that we have something to ride in until we get something else and it would get better. I continued to pray that this wouldn't affect them. You never know how kids will react to situations. But throughout the ordeal they got better. I lost my car but God sent my brothers to be a blessing to me. Through the months I didn't have a vehicle I never went without one, and they didn't make me feel like I was a bother. I tried to give them money to show that I appreciated their help but they wouldn't take it. I went from worrying about how I was going to get back and forth to having peace. Even though it wasn't my car it could have been that I didn't have anyone to turn to. I didn't have a way to go and I could have lost my job and lost the place I was living at. But God provided for me in this time. I understood that my situation was bad but could have turned out to be a lot worse. It is always a blessing to be a blessing to others. At one point in my life I was able to be a blessing but now I had to be on the receiving end. Even though you want to always be the one to give its ok to get help from others. If you can bless someone be a blessing because you never know when you might need someone to step in and be that blessing for you. If I had of let my pride get in the way I probably would have lost my job and my apartment. Just simply asking for help and explaining my situation caused me to go from no car to having two cars. I was able to keep my job and save a little money. Remember that you're not the only one that goes through situations and there are people that are willing to help you if you let them. Always be grateful and thankful for the people that God has placed in your life to help you along the way. Proverbs 11:25 *"Whoever brings blessing will be enriched, and one who waters will himself be watered."*

MY PRAYER

Dear God,

I am coming to you thanking you for all that you have done for us. Even when we were at our lowest point you never left us. The times that we lost our vehicles the times that we might have lost our homes you never left us. Thank you for sending angels our way to help us in our time of need. Continue to bless us and keep us and let us be a blessing to others one day. Let us be able to learn from the things that we've been through and be able to grow from it. Bless us with an overflow of abundant blessings so that we can help others. We pray all these blessings in your son Jesus name,

Amen.

YOUR SCRIPTURES

Romans 12:13 "Contribute to the needs of the saints and seek to show hospitality."

Acts 20:35 "In all things I have shown you that by working hard in this way we must help the weak and remember the words of the Lord Jesus, how he himself said, "it is more blessed to give than to receive."

Luke 6:38 "Give, and it will be given to you. Good measure, pressed down, shaken together, running over, will be put into your lap. For with the measure you use it will be measured back to you."

What can I change in my life?

_____

_____

_____

_____

_____

_____

What are my goals to achieve it?

_____

_____

_____

_____

_____

_____

_____

CHAPTER 10

Accepting your gift...

I knew as a young child that I was different. I could feel and see things different from others. I sometimes would feel emotional but couldn't explain it. As I got older I learned to suppress things and deal with life as it was. I enjoyed marriage, but it took God taking and stripping me from everything until I surrendered to Him. I knew with the repetitive events in my life that God was making me birth my gift. Sometimes, we must be broken down to discover our real purpose. I knew that I had the gift of reaching people and I loved to talk and listen to others. I especially liked uplifting and helping others every chance I got...I didn't think it would be to speak and motivate a mass of people. I really believe that God has a purpose for everything and through His plan we will succeed and win. When I was younger I remember that I used to have a chill feeling that would come over me when something bad was about to happen. I didn't know how to explain it to anyone and people will think that you are losing your mind if tell them...Usually, something would happen that wasn't good. I would be terrified. I would cry and simply didn't know what to say to explain why I was feeling this way. So that no one would think that I was crazy or commit me to a mental institution, I started keeping these feelings to myself. I prayed to God and asked Him to take it away...but He didn't. He gave me the strength to deal with it until I could understand what it really was. Now that I look back, it was just the anointing that was on my life at the time. As an adult you get comfortable and just deal with the feelings. It's such a true statement that you will never be yourself until you surrender and find your purpose. I was truly struggling with what He wanted me to do. I knew He wanted me to impact people with my life but I didn't know how I was going to do it. How could my story change someone else's life? How do I even set out to accomplish the vision that He wants me to have? All God kept telling me to do was speak and let your voice be heard. It doesn't matter who thinks that it's impossible or who thinks that you're crazy. You're no different from anyone else. I have chosen you to go on this journey not anyone else. I have anointed you to speak to various people, share your story and inspire them on their journey. God never promised that the task would be easy, but He did promise me that I had a series of stories that needed to be shared with the world. I am walking to fulfil His promise. The journey is not easy and there are many people that question and doubt me. This journey has been tough and sometimes I felt like I was alone. I had to realize that I had to be alone so that I could advance to the next level. I had to move in a direction where I could allow my growth to expand. I had to try new things and be willing to acknowledge that some people will not understand my walk. They will think that I am crazy and that I will not be able to succeed. Those people are just obstacles to distract me from doing my purpose. I will not allow things and people to interfere in what God has planned. I know that as I do His work He will put a protection around me that no one can touch. You have to leave some people behind because they will hinder you from getting to your next level. They will not understand your drive. They will not understand why you are so driven! The norm is ok for them but if you are called to do something other than the norm then some people will not understand. They will accuse you of trying to live a life that *they think* you can't have. One thing about some people that I have learned is they will talk about you only because they don't have the courage that you have to succeed. I have learned to drown out all negative energy that may come my way. I am ultimately in control of what negativity I allow in my life. It was all in the process of changing my thoughts and defining what my purpose was and that in turn changed my mindset. I now know what my purpose is and now it's my duty to fulfill it. I know by walking in faith and doing what I am called to do will help others in their walk of life.

MY PRAYER

Dear God,

I come to you asking that you continue to bless and watch over everyone that wants to be close to you. Help them to be obedient to their calling so that your purpose will be fulfilled. It will help people to live a better life and a more fulfilling life. Let them be able to distinguish between what their purpose is and what isn't. Also, bless me to be strong and to continue to do the work you have requested of me. These and other blessings in your son Jesus name we pray,

Amen.

YOUR SCRIPTURE

Psalms 138:8 "The Lord will fulfill his purpose for me; your steadfast love, O lord, endures forever. Do not forsake the work of your hands."

Romans 8:28 "And we know that for those who love God all things work together for good, for those who are called according to his purpose."

Matthew 5:16 "In the same way, let your light shine before others, so that they may see your good works and give glory to your Father who is in heaven."

What can I change in my life?

_____
_____
_____
_____
_____
_____

What are my goals to achieve it?

_____
_____
_____
_____
_____
_____

CHAPTER 11

ADHD, Anxiety & Depression

Being divorced single parent has brought a lot of changes in my life. Even with that, both of my kids have suffered from either anxiety or ADHD/ADD. That alone has been difficult at times. Trying to maintain the strength to keep both kids in a position to win in life while being strong has been a struggle but I have managed to do an awesome job in this. I never want my kids to be defeated by anything that they can conquer. So that means I had to get some strength when I was weak because they needed me. Sometimes you must be strong when you think you don't have any fight to be strong. Philippians 4:13 *"I can do all things through him who gives me strength."* Isaiah 40:29 *"He gives strength to the weary and increases the power of the weak."* God gives you the strength that you think you don't have. When you have children that have issues people on the outside really don't understand. And then there are the looks that you get because they think that your kids run over you. There will always be some type of outside chatter that you know people have said about your situation yet they never have experienced what you endure. At one point I was getting angry because I thought people were so rude and the things that I wanted to say, I didn't. At times I would just remove myself from situations so that I wouldn't respond in the wrong way. Then I realized that until a person understands or has lived in your situation they wouldn't understand. I went into deep prayer on how to handle the situation with people. I got clarity on how to respond to people and how to make them realize that every child is different. There would be times that I would have a hard day at home. I would resolve the problem with one child then the other one would have an issue. I would literally go to my room and cry and pray. I asked God to help me be the best parent that I could be. I would ask Him to show me how to deal with these issues. Then we would be ok and go somewhere as a family. My son would sometimes have a social issue and we would be back at square one. The biggest part was the looks I would get and the stares. They didn't understand that he sometimes had social attacks. The same thing would happen if we would be somewhere and then my daughter would start crying because of the weather. People were looking like she is too big to be acting like that. They didn't understand that she has panic attacks and anxiety. So, I got to the point where I didn't want to go around people to keep me from getting upset. God gave me clarity one day that my kids are great kids. They are my kids and people that look and judge don't understand my situation. They have issues of their own and they can't judge you. After that moment I really didn't get bothered about how people felt. I didn't care how they felt when I told them that every child is different. I felt like a burden had been lifted off me. As the years progressed, things have gotten better for my kids. We still have our moments of melt downs, and we have had our crying and fearful moments.

I applaud my kids for being overcomers of a lot of things that use to take control of them. There was a time that when it rained I didn't know rather I would be able to work or be waiting on the phone call to come pick my daughter up from school. I thank God for placing great teachers in her life that would help her cope with the situation. They understood and didn't judge or give her a hard time. I would always let them know at the beginning of the year of the problems that we encountered. It would be so bad that after a storm, family members would call to check on us to see how she did. My son, despite of his ADHD/ADD he would be strong for her on that aspect and comfort her as well. I thank God for the change and growth in both my kids. My son has suffered a lot with school as far as his learning is concerned, but he has made a great improvement. It was a time that I had to call several meetings because I didn't want him to be set up for failure. He never made less than a 75% average, but I knew that he could do better. Just a few improvements through the school year made a tremendous difference in his grades. In my opinion, it only takes a parent taking the time to address issues that can be done a little differently at school. The communication between the school and home went very well. I was so aggressive as a parent in making sure he didn't struggle...It made all the difference in his academics. I had to get tutors, but whatever measures it took to make sure he understood I made sure it was done. As parents, sometimes we don't pay attention to our kids like we should. We don't take the time to see if there is anything they're struggling in or having a hard time understanding. It's not always that your kids are bad. It's not always that they don't want to learn. Sometimes, it's the method of teaching. If it is addressed, different things can be done to help your kids improve their grades. I would encourage all parents to be more involved in their kid's school and social life. You don't want to ever overlook something that you might just think is a small problem. I talk with my kids and tell them that they can be open with me. I always ask them how their day was and I let them know they can come to me for anything no matter what. Even if someone threatens them they can still come to me. It is important to have a line of communication so that they feel comfortable in discussing issues. I have learned that through this method they feel free to talk to me about things that bother them or things they think aren't fair. We shouldn't always be so caught up in fussing or not having a little time to let them speak freely on issues. It's healthy to think of how the child feels. They are not always able to explain themselves and then they begin to turn to other things that could cause more harm. I have made it an important factor to make sure that we have family time. This is important for kids that struggle with stress, anxiety and ADHD. Even though our life might be busy we should still take the time to discuss issues and show our kids that we love them. Everything in life is not perfect...I found that time spent with your kids is more valuable than spending lots of money. You will find that it helps your kids with issues that they might be struggling with. I know if you are like me, being a single parent and busy, you think that you don't have time to sit down and cater to your kids. But it's not catering...It's therapy for you and your kids. I noticed that my kids would share things with me that I found to be insignificant, but it was a big deal for them. As parents we must learn that we are not perfect and everything we do isn't necessarily correct. We should be open to learning from our kids. The times are constantly changing from when we grew up. We need to adapt to a new way of communicating and helping our kids to deal with the issues of the world. As a parent with a kid with ADHD and ADD I learned that sometimes things are hard for them. Some kids feel as if they are not accepted and loved and they sometimes don't interact well with other kids and tend to want to play alone. Some kids think that they are strange. I learned that some kids don't understand and sometimes can be rude and mean. But as a parent I had to learn how to correct others behavior and explain that every child has their own unique talents. I also had to explain to my child that he is special and a unique jewel. I constantly teach my kids that they have beautiful talents and no matter how people feel about them that they will always be God's beautiful creation. He made them to be a priceless jewel and they have talents that no one can take from them. We should always make sure we talk to our kids and let them know how proud we are of them and how they can accomplish anything in life if they put their minds to it. Your children need your time and attention as much as your job and any other extra activities that you might have. What you pour into your kids is much needed. Things that we do they watch but the simple things like time is so important.

Depression...

Millions of people live with depression and anxiety in the world. How they cope with it is different. Some people are embarrassed of the fact that they have this issue. Some people feel as if they don't have to take medicine to cope with these things. They are ashamed to let people know or feel as if people are going to look at them in a certain way. It is so common now that with life stresses I believe everybody has some form of depression or anxiety at times. I dealt with anxiety as a little girl ...As I grew up, I learned to cope with it the best way I could. As life goes on, things get harder... Challenges get harder and sometimes one thing can take you over the edge; for me, that was my divorce. Some people are depressed and don't even know it. And if you know someone that's in this situation, try to help them. Just being a listening ear is all the help they may need. Sometimes, they may feel as if no one is able to help. Don't be so critical of their situations because you never know if that's the last thing that will take them on over the edge to do something to themselves. I always try to be a listening ear to people. I always encourage people to take time to go sit at a park away from daily life struggles and meditate. Monday through Friday I always go to the park and sit about 30 minutes. I meditate and just take in some of the things of life that God has created. It's away from work. It's away from home. It's a place you could just simply breathe and enjoy life. Sometimes that's the only thing you need, a place to get away from daily situations. I truly believe that if I didn't do anything about my situation when I was diagnosed I probably would have been admitted into someone's hospital. I thought I had it under control but my body was showing signs of failure. Some of the same people that tell you that you can do this on your own are the same ones that can't do it on their own. These are the same people that if you lose your mind, your family, your kids or do something crazy to yourself, will be the same ones that gossip about you. Only you are in control of your health and well-being. You are worth living and taking care of yourself. Don't let depression and anxiety take over your life. Find avenues and ways to relieve stress and enjoy time with God. You'll be surprised about the peace that you can get just taking a walk in the park and God speaking with you. Being able to cope with life is a struggle sometimes but have faith and you will be able to do it. Isaiah 41:10 *"So do not fear, for I am with you; do not be dismayed, for I am your God. I will strengthen you and help you; I will uphold you with my righteous hand."*

MY PRAYER FOR YOU

Dear God,

We come to you in all praises. Thank you for our gift that you gave us on earth. Thanks for allowing us to be able to be parents. Continue to bless over us that we are wise and able to bring our kids up in a way that you would be pleased. Also bless our kids to be protected from the things that will cause hurt, harm, and danger. Let them be a light in this world that will carry what you have planned for them. I continue to pray that they will continue to keep you close to their hearts and that they know that if they have you they will not fail. These and all other blessings in your son Jesus name I pray,

Amen.

YOUR SCRIPTURES

Proverbs 22:6 "Start children off on the way they should go, and even when they are old they will not turn from it."

Proverbs 1:8 "Listen, my son, to your father's instruction and do not forsake your mother's teaching."

What can I change in my life?

_____

_____

_____

_____

_____

_____

What are my goals to achieve it?

_____

_____

_____

_____

_____

_____

_____

_____

Chapter 12

Raising kids

My journey has not been easy as a single parent, but it has been rewarding. I have learned to endure things alone. I have seen my kids question me about things that I couldn't control. There have been times that if only their father was present, we both could sit down and explain certain things. But I had to do it alone and I always reassured them that both me and their father loved them. I tried to keep that going in their mind even though sometimes they would question the love from their father. My son was a year old when their father and I separated. He never got the chance to experience the two-parent household scenario like my daughter. I didn't realize that it would have been so hard on him. My daughter experienced all these emotions when we first went through our separation and divorce. She was often upset and cried. She couldn't understand why we couldn't just live together like before. I had to go to the school functions when they wanted their father there. When it was a function for only dads I had to step in the gap. It was an experience that was indescribable. It felt awkward to be a mom there instead of the dad, but it had to be done. The kids didn't want anyone else but me to take them if their dad couldn't take them. I learn to disregard what others thought. I knew that it had to be harder on them than it was for me and that they had to feel ten times worse than me. I knew that they had to hear the questions from their friends asking why their dad wasn't there. I thought of their feelings and learned to subside mine. It was all about making them feel important and comfortable in a situation that we couldn't change. Even though at times they felt hurt at these functions, they would always hold their heads up high and never showed sadness in front of others. I would be extremely proud of them. They learned to cope with each situation as it came there way. I learned a lot from my kids and they learned from me. As I watched how they would respond to events like this showed me that I could conquer fears and not worry about how others think of me. John 14:27 *"Peace I leave with you. I do not give to you as the world gives. Do not let your hearts be troubled and do not be afraid."* One day after I dropped my daughter off at dance my son and I was riding down the road and he asked me a hurtful question. He turned to me and says "Mom, does my dad love me?" I told him yes and asked why he would ask that type of question. He said "Because he never wants to be around me and he never lived in the house with me like he did my sister..." I explained to him that he wasn't the reason for his dad and I not being together. He started to cry and asked more questions. He asked me if I thought that his dad thinks he talks too much or thought that he was weird. I told him that he doesn't...Then he asked why his father is with other people and not him. During that time his father was dating someone and she had a son around my son's age. I immediately told him that he loves him no matter what. We just stay too far away for you to see him every day. I told him never compare yourself to others when it comes to your dad. You will always be number one in his life. But those are only words in a child's eyes. He looked at me and started crying. I held him and we prayed. Every day I would pray that God would let him see that his dad does love him and to let them get closer. The only thing that I could do at that time was comfort him. Those days would come and go but this day was by far the worst! I prayed for strength over my son and that he would be strong and mighty throughout this struggle and that God would allow him to have peace. 1 Peter 5:7 *"Cast all your anxiety on him because he cares for you."* It had been two years since my kids seen their dad. It was something that shouldn't have never happened. I noticed that my son would continue to ask about his dad. He would make comments like "I do this like my dad" as if he had seen him. I knew that it had started to affect him. God had spoken to me plenty of times telling me to take my kids to Florida to visit their father. My response was "No, I'm not doing that... I think that is so crazy because he can come visit them. He can visit them whenever he wants to. It shouldn't be any reason I should have to drive to Orlando to take the kids. He goes everywhere else he can come see them." God kept speaking to me saying this isn't about you. I want you to do this for your kids. My response was "I understand God, but why should I have to do all the work. I have them every day and do everything on my own and now you want me to go out my way to do this. I don't understand why you keep putting so much on me..." But He said until you do what I say there will be no peace. I struggled with this for a while. I finally decided to take them. It was the best thing I ever did. My kids were so excited to see their dad. My son ran to him and jumped in his arms. It brought so much joy to my heart. It was something special about that moment that was undeniable. We went to lunch together and the kids spent time with him. When I met him to pick up the kids they were so happy. I could tell that it was much needed time with their father. They were happy that we were getting along. When we got home they talked about what they did with their dad. It was very helpful and healthy. I immediately noticed a change in attitudes, especially my son. It was as if it was something that he had been waiting for forever. So why I was questioning God, He was working the situation out to make it where we could be good co-parents. I really think that co-parenting is a great option if you can put aside all differences and come to an agreement for your kids' sake. It's not about what you've been through with that person when it comes to developing a relationship to raise your kids. I think that fathers should play their part as a parent as well as the mother. If you can co-parent, allow it to happen. Not only will it bring about a healthy relationship between the parents, but it's more beneficial and healthy for the kids. They see unity and know that despite anything, their parents will work together and make sure they are ok and both parents love them. Even though I drove seven hours so that they could see their dad (thinking that it would encourage a change in him) I suddenly realized that it was not about us, but about my kids. As of today, I'm still open for co-parenting, but it also takes two to co-parent. One person can't do all the work. The other parent must be willing to sacrifice and meet the other parent half way. The only thing that you can do whenever a parent chooses not to participate in a child's life is to leave it in God's hands. After you have prayed about it, there is nothing more you can do. If co-parenting is not an option, pray that God allows good mentors to be around your kids. Pray that God protects them and fills the void that is not fulfilled by the other parent. This is the only thing that you can do other than letting your child know that they are not at fault. A lot of times we get so caught up in our own life and feelings that we do not think about how it affects the children. If possible, always keep an open mind and let your kids enjoy both parents. If by chance one parent is not cooperating and is not willing to be a part of their child's life, continue to pray and do what you can as a single parent. God will answer your prayers. He can send someone else to fill those shoes and they will result in being the perfect role model as a father or mother figure in their lives. Just know if you are doing everything that you can God will reward you. It is up to us to raise productive, smart and loving kids. You just got to see the bigger picture and make peace so that the relationship works. James 3:18 *"Peacemakers who sow in peace reap a harvest of righteousness."*

MY PRAYER

Dear God,

We come to you with a humble heart knowing that we are not perfect but strive to do the best work we can for you. Lord help us to see that our kids are the most important concern in broken homes. If the parents aren't in the same household let them be awesome co-parents. Please bring more healthy relationships between parents so that their kids can be in a healthier environment. Kids that have a parent that is not participating in their life please fill the gap. Let them not feel lonely and let them not think that their parents do not love them. These and all other blessings in your son Jesus name I pray,

Amen.

YOUR SCRIPTURE

Philippians 4:7 "And the peace of God, which transcends all understanding, will guard your hearts and your minds in Christ Jesus."

Romans 14:19 "Let us therefore make every effort to do what leads to peace and to mutual edification."

Romans 12: 8 "If possible, as far as it depends on you, live at peace with everyone."

What can I change in my life?

_____

_____

_____

_____

_____

_____

What are my goals to achieve it?

_____

_____

_____

_____

_____

_____

_____

Chapter 13

Life decisions...

I remember a few years back when I had to make a life decision on my own. I had been suffering with pain and my abdomen had started to swell. I went to the doctor and they told me that I had a cyst and that it could prevent me from having more children if I had it removed. I lived with that cyst for several years. It was sometimes uncomfortable, but I chose not to do anything at the time because I thought that one day I may have more kids. I didn't want to make that decision so soon in my life. I was hoping to be married and then make that decision with my significant other. This decision would be life-changing for me because I love kids and I always wanted to be in the position to have them. When I first found out they told me that it wasn't a large cyst. I could manage it and the pain wasn't too bad and unbearable. Plus, it wasn't a decision that I had to make fast. As the years went on, the cyst got larger. The pain was more excruciating and it looked as if I was 4 months pregnant. I returned to my doctor and he suggested surgery and I really wasn't ready for that. It was something that I had to strongly think about because it was a life-changing decision. If I had the surgery it would mean that I couldn't have any more kids. The cyst was so large that the doctor suggested I have a hysterectomy. I really wasn't prepared for that so I asked him if I could have a second opinion. I was referred to a specialist. We stayed in prayer before I went to the specialist. I still didn't want to deal with the fact that I had to make that decision. The day finally arrived for my appointment. I was very nervous and was hoping that he would give me better news than what I had before. I still wanted to have the option to be able to have more kids. I felt like that was something that could potentially run my future husband away. Well, I sat in that room and waited on him to come in to speak with me. I began reminiscing on the fact that it was a time that I couldn't have kids. I didn't want the Lord to think that I was being selfish. But at the same time, I at least wanted the option to have more. When he came in the room he gave me my options. He described in detail the surgery that I would have and that he would try to save my uterus. He continued to tell me that if I did decide to do this, that I risked the chance of losing my life on the table. He looked at me and suggested that I shouldn't do it. But the ultimate decision was mine. He said that you have two beautiful kids and most people need this surgery because they don't have any. As I sat there and listened to him I decided that the surgery to save my uterus was not worth me losing my life on the table. So, I decided to have the hysterectomy. I thought about my two kids and leaving them without a mother and that was not an option. To me that would have been so selfish. I thank God for allowing me to have a boy and a girl. I no longer try to throw a pity party for myself. I immediately started thanking God for allowing me to have the two kids that I have. I started reminiscing on the kids and I asked God that whoever He places in my life let them love my kids as they love you. The day arrived that I had to have the surgery. I thought that I was mentally prepared. I was ready for the surgery and I was ready to get it over with. I arrived at the hospital very early. As I laid back I began to get nervous and started thinking crazy thoughts. I was afraid that I wasn't going to wake up from the surgery. When the doctor came to talk to me I was in a panic and they immediately started administering drugs. Psalms 56: 3 *"When I am afraid, I put my trust in you."* All I remember is waking up into excruciating pain. The surgery was overwhelming, but everything was fine. I stayed in the hospital for two days. I left a day early because of my advancements. But the first day the pain was so terrible that I almost couldn't take it. They said that it was normal. I had a pump that was broken and they had to replace it. This pump was administering drugs to me and keeping me from being in pain. But I was very determined to get out of there so I began to start walking earlier than what was expected. The doctors said they were very amazed at my progress. I was able to go home very soon but when I was home I had a very hard time. Being home alone was very hard even though I had my family- it wasn't the same as having a spouse with you. I do appreciate everything that my family did for me. But sometimes I felt like I was being a bother to them. My family has done so much for me and I could never repay them back. I couldn't drive for two weeks. And it took almost six weeks before my body could get back into the same routine. As I laid there I was beginning to get closer and closer to God. I was able to read my Bible to study more of His Word. I was able to listen to Him as He spoke to me. During this time, I began writing...that's when the vision was given to me, but I didn't follow up on it. Every day that I was home my strength got better and I felt better about the decision that I had made. I was glad to still be alive and be able to take care of my kids. I was thanking Him for all the blessings that He has given me and telling myself to not be so ungrateful. You don't always understand the things that you go through, but He will soon reveal all in due time. If I had not of had that surgery, I would have experienced more medical problems. So, I thank God for everything that He has allowed me to go through to help others. Isaiah 41:10 *"So do not fear, for I am with you, do not be dismayed, for I am your God. I will strengthen you and help you: I will uphold you with my righteous right hand."*

MY PRAYER

Dear God,

Thank you for providing for us in our time of need. Thanks for allowing us to be strong when we think we are not and for letting us see our way when we are blind. Continue to guide us and to help us make the right decisions. Let our hearts be humble to your answers. Let us understand that everything that looks bad really is working out for our good. Continue to bless everybody's health and strength. I pray for the people that cannot conceive kids. Let them know that it might not be your will for them to conceive but that they can help others. Let them see other options and that there are other kids that need parents. Let them have the strength to understand that everything works out according to your wishes in your command. These and all blessings we ask in your son Jesus name,

Amen.

YOUR SCRIPTURE

1 Peter 5:7 "Cast all your anxiety on him because he cares for you."

Psalm 119:71 "It was good for me to be afflicted so that I might learn your discreet."

Psalm 120:1 "I called on the Lord in my distress, and he answers me."

What can I change in my life?

What are my goals to achieve it?

Chapter 14

Find who you are...

Some people have lived their whole entire life not knowing who they are. And some have gotten conformed to the norm of everyday living. They do things and cater to other people's needs and simply just don't know their purpose. Some don't even know if they are in a verbally abusive relationship because they've been in it for so long. Most will make others happy and don't know how to make themselves happy. In some cases, when couples have been married for so long they try to please their mate and forget who they really are. This is what happened to me during my marriage. I lived to please my husband...If he was happy, I was happy. I felt that was my duty as his wife to make sure that he was pleased and satisfied. But along the way I lost who I really was. I didn't have extra activities or much of a social life. Everything was pretty much wrapped around being a wife and mother. I didn't have any hobbies. The only thing that I wanted to do was have a family, raise my kids and make sure that I was the perfect wife. He wasn't making me do it, but that's the home I built. He grew accustomed to that lifestyle and wasn't use to me doing anything different or going places with other people. I don't regret the things that I've done in my marriage. It made me who I am today. If I had any regrets it would be that I didn't find what made me happy. I didn't do the things that I wanted to do and I certainly didn't realize I was experiencing verbal abuse. There were times that I wanted to do or try things that were different, but he made me feel like it wasn't important or that it was a very dumb or stupid idea. Whenever I spoke around him, I would sometimes speak low so that he couldn't hear me. He would often tell me that I needed to speak up or try and correct how I talked. He would even cut me off when

I said something and he would belittle me...it wasn't all the time, but enough to where I didn't feel comfortable speaking around others. I can remember on several occasions when we were out and when I spoke, he gave me the look of "What are you talking about?" It was a look of embarrassment. I couldn't believe that he would correct me in front of other people. Listen, this is a situation that if you are in you need to correct it as soon as it starts. My problem was that I had let it go on for so many years that it was my normal. This feeling was something that stuck with me and I didn't like it. I am in a better mindset now and in a better environment. I have moved on with my life and I suggest that everyone finds what makes them happy. If you can't express yourself around that person then maybe that's not a healthy relationship. I have found a lot of my hidden talents, uncovered new hobbies and find that I have knowledge that people find interesting. Since I have discovered who I am and know my purpose, I am able to express myself and speak confidently in front of others. The things that I have embedded in me I've learned to express it and let it go. I also know that no one's perfect and that if I make a mistake in my English then that's ok. I shouldn't feel bad about anything that I've said or done and no one should make anyone feel as if they are not worthy. Your opinions matter and the things that you say matter. Your hobbies are great and they're just as important as the next person's. Never let anyone make you feel that you're not great. If you end a toxic relationship with someone who belittles you and makes you feel like you're not worthy enough for speaking, and that your hobbies are not great enough to be expressed then you need to reevaluate your situation. Don't live your life for someone else. You both have a life to live and both of you should be able to express yourselves. Find who you are and don't live your life in fear. John 14:27 *"Peace I leave with you, my peace I give you. I do not give to you as the world gives. Do not let your hearts be troubled and do not be afraid."*

MY PRAYER

Dear God,

Thank you for allowing me to understand that I am a beautiful person that should be respected. My words do matter and my thoughts are courageous. Thank you for showing me that fear should not be in my vocabulary. Please show others that they are important. Please show them that they can be themselves and that you created everybody in a different way so that they can be a light in the world. Let them know that they shouldn't be afraid to speak or do anything that makes them happy. Show them the difference between verbal abuse and just being corrected. Please surround them around people that can build them up. These blessings we pray in your son Jesus name,

Amen.

YOUR SCRIPTURE

Deuteronomy 31:6 "Be strong and courageous. Do not be afraid or terrified of them, for the Lord your God goes with you; he will never leave you nor forsake you."

1 Corinthians 16:13 "Be on your guard; stand firm in the faith; be courageous; Be strong."

What can I change in my life?

_____

_____

_____

_____

_____

_____

What are my goals to achieve it?

_____

_____

_____

_____

_____

_____

_____

_____

Chapter 15

Worth

Have you ever thought to yourself why even try? Have you ever thought that you would never make it to the next day? Does it seem like the harder you try the more you get set back? Or, maybe like you're in a box by yourself and you're just suffocating? Or, it seems like no one really understands what you're going through? Well, I've been in a place where I even questioned my existence. I wondered was it any need for me to even be here. I was constantly depressed, constantly crying, and drowning in debt. It seemed like I could never get a break to just sit back, breathe and enjoy life. I felt like I was a failure not only to myself, but to my children. I would talk to people about my life and tell them that I was frustrated and tired. I would get the same response. Everyone thought that I was so strong and that I was just blowing hot air. But what they really didn't know was that I was on the verge of going off the deep end. I questioned my existence. The only thing that kept me from being suicidal were my two beautiful kids. Even though I felt like I was failing them I knew that they were depending on me. I knew that I was their only strength. I knew that when they saw me they didn't see my verge of a breakdown. All they saw was a mother that was simply loving them and providing for them. One day I remember laying in my bed crying. It was an overwhelming day for me. It was a stressful day at work, I had to do a lot of ripping and running for the kids, bills were hitting me left and right, and I was just trying to figure out how to provide. I had years and years of buildup just smothering me...I was tired of doing things on my own. I laid in my bed and I said to God I'm not sure what your plan is...I know that I am not this terrible of a person to be going through so many trials and tribulations. I prayed for kids, you gave me kids and now you're making me go through things as a single parent...You're making me struggle through all these situations and making me go through all this depression. I'm not sure what I've done that was so bad that you would make me go through all this and make me lose my mind. I don't know how much more of this I can take and I am going to need you to help me. I cried for hours and hours and hours. I literally made myself sick. The next day, I didn't feel any better. I questioned God again. I was angry with Him because I didn't understand what He was trying to do. I was caught between I'm giving up and I am going to walk away from everything, put my kids in the car and just ride until we can't ride anymore. I told God that I was going to need Him to just tell me what I'm doing that is so wrong. For a solid week I was shut off from everything. I didn't want to talk to anyone and everything seemed to frustrate me. Every night I went to bed I would just cry myself to sleep. One night when I was talking to God and asked Him again, "Why me? Why can't I just be happy? Why are you putting me through so much pain, stress, and constant struggles? Do you not know that this affects not only me, but the kids that you gave me? I'm not understanding why...Wasn't it enough that my marriage wasn't successful and that I got to do this on my own?" The answer that God gave me was "I'm making you a leader." I thought to myself "What do you mean you making me a leader? What I'm going through? I'm tired. I'm stressed. There's no leadership in that! So, I'm going to need you to be clear." The only answer God kept giving me was "I'm making you a leader." I pondered about that until I fell asleep. When I woke up, I asked the same question and I still got the same answer. I went throughout my day and He spoke to me again. "I am making you stronger than before because leaders need to be strong." I'm sitting here thinking to myself I don't have any money. I am struggling to make ends meet. I'm ripping and running from school to school activities and I really don't understand how any of that can have any form of leadership. Then I began to pray. I asked God the same question. He said, "I already spoke to you child, I am making you a leader." And it was just like it was the first time He spoke to me. I automatically got a calm feeling over me because this time He gave me a scripture to read. James 1:2- 4 *"Consider it pure joy, my brothers and sisters, whenever you face trials of many kinds, because you know that the testing of your faith produces perseverance. Let perseverance finish its work so that you may be mature and complete, not lacking anything."* Now out of those verses there were two words that stood out to me. Perseverance and many. The Word said that there will be many trials not just one. While I was just focused on the situation that I was going through, He made me reflect through the years and all the trials and tribulations that I had been through. The definition of perseverance is continued effort to do or achieve something despite difficulties, failure, or opposition. I looked back over the last few years that led to this point... I had questioned God, cried every night for a solid week in my box and thought about that scripture. He told me He was building me up to be a leader. Not just for that situation, but for all my situations so that I can help others. I immediately started crying tears of happiness instead of tears of failure. He only prepares those that He knows will be able to persevere through their trials without giving up. He had to bring me through all these situations so that I can be the leader that I am today. That I can be someone that can bridge the gap for someone that is not strong enough to see their way. I thank God for all my trials and all my tribulations that I went through because if it had not been for that failed marriage, those failed relationships, and the point where I couldn't take it anymore, I wouldn't be able to be who I am today. We need to focus on what God wants us to do instead of what we want to do. We wouldn't be going through so many trials if we would spend our time focusing on the things that He wants us to do. If you're at the point where you just can't take it anymore, feel like you're about to lose everything, and you just want to just go and disappear, you need to turn to God. The best time to be in His presence is when you have only Him. He will show you the things that you need to be doing, but you must be willing to accept the knowledge that He's giving you. The things that He wants us to do is not necessarily the things that we have planned for our lives. He promised to provide for all our needs. But we must allow Him to work on us so that we can be the best person to others. Giving up is the easy way out. If we're going to give up, why do we continue to ask God for direction? If things were so easy in life then everyone would be doing the same thing. God makes people to be leaders for a reason. So, the next time you're going through a situation, remember that only the strong survive and ask God to show you your purpose.

MY PRAYER

Dear God,

We come to you asking you to give hope to everyone that is going through trials and tribulations. Bless the ones that are feeling like they're stuck in a box and suffocating. I bring to you the ones that feel like they can't make it one more minute or one more second without exploding. Let them get to a place where they can only see you God. Give them the wisdom to see that the things that they're going through is to make them stronger. Let them have perseverance to continue to strive through their situation and become leaders. Lord when they make it through their trials and tribulations I pray that they understand that they are to help others. Let them know that they're not alone in their situation and that someone is depending on them. When they are weak and they feel like they're not able to make it let them know that's when they need to listen to you more God. These blessings we pray in your son Jesus name,

Amen.

YOUR SCRIPTURE

James 1:12 "Blessed is the one who preserves under trial because, having stood the test, that person will receive the crown of life that the Lord has promised to those who love him."

Romans 8:28 "And we know that in all things God works for the good of those who love him, who have been called according to his purpose."

Romans 5:3 - 5 "Not only so, but we also glory in our sufferings, because we know that suffering produces perseverance; perseverance, character; and character, hope. And hope does not put us to shame, because God's love has been poured out into our hearts through the Holy Spirit, who has been given to us."

What can I change in my life?

_____
_____
_____
_____
_____

What are my goals to achieve it?

_____
_____
_____
_____
_____
_____

CHAPTER 16

Naked in Christ

The word naked has many definitions and usually tends to have a negative effect. The definition I'm referring to is having feelings or behavior undisguised. Strive to be free within yourself...It doesn't matter what you have done in your past, the hurt you've been through, the anger that you held, or what people have done to you. You are free from what other people might think of you or how they feel about you. I often think of it this way, we come to Christ with all our baggage and dirty laundry, but he wants to cleanse and restore us. He must strip us from all the past and make us new again. After we have tried everything that we could we must throw away our old ways and change for the better. When you do this, you might have to leave old friends, family members and get a whole new circle of friends. God wants us to be renewed in Him so that He can cleanse us for the better to help others. Psalm 51:10-12 *"Create in me a clean heart, O God, and renew a steadfast spirit within me."* Once you change, that's when the devil really goes to work. He knows that once you change, you'll be able to reach other people and restore them as well. So therefore, the enemy will come and attack you. It will appear as though every corner that you turn there is a problem. It will appear as if every door that you open that there is someone standing there trying to stop you. But just know that this is happening only because you're closer to Christ than ever before. Just know that you're closer to rejoicing and enjoying what God has for you. Do not let people or distractions keep you from going forward in Christ. Don't let it keep you from doing the things that you need to do to accomplish the goals in your life. Those things are just stumbling blocks to deter you from your happiness. Remember, God wants people that are in the world to come unto Him and change their ways. It gets harder and harder to block out some of the enemy's attacks, but just know that when things come knocking at your door, it's only a distraction. When you're living for God He comes first and there will be no shame in representing Him! You don't have to go around talking about God all the time to everyone. If you live the right way everyone will recognize Christ in you. The way that you carry yourself, the way that you act, and the way that you respond to situations will be totally different than before. Some people tend to think that once you find God you just turn away from the world. But that is not so...In fact, you're more in tune with the world, you're just wise enough to make decisions that will please Christ. You can be happy, live life and still love Christ all at the same time. Don't let anyone think that because you choose to live a different lifestyle and take a different path that you're strange. You are different only because now you carry the light of Him. You know that His way is the only way that will help you along this journey. One of the biggest mistakes that I find some people making is worrying about what people think about them after they find Christ. When really this is the time that you should be enjoying and not worrying about what others think of you. If you're living your life the way that you should, those who are truly your friends will be there with you through this journey. I always say you can't make anyone do anything or feel a certain way that they don't want to feel. You can tell them your opinion, but it's up to them to make the decision. After you have done your part it's out of your hands and out of your control. I do know that God does not want you to be ashamed of Him. When you come to Him, He wants you to be sincere and open. If you're struggling with life situations, just try Jesus...He will never fail you. Jesus wants you to live a life of abundance and happiness!

MY PRAYER

Dear God,

We come to you asking that you cleanse us and strip us from all things that are not right in your eyesight. Let us be strong enough to defend the evil ways of this world. Let us be able to decipher good from evil. Help us to be sincere and pure when we come to you. Help us to be the light to others so that they see the goodness of you through us. Protect us from our enemies as we get closer to you and thank you for letting our enemies be our stepping stool to get closer to you. These blessings we pray in Jesus name,

Amen.

YOUR SCRIPTURE

John 14:6 "Jesus said to him," I am the way, and the truth, and the life. No one comes to the father except through me."

John 14:27 "Peace I leave with you; my peace I give to you. Not as the world gives do I give to you. Let not your hearts be troubled, neither let them be afraid."

1 Timothy 2:5 "For there is one God, and there is one mediator between God and Men, the man Christ Jesus."

1 John 1:9 "If we confess our sins, he is faithful and just to forgive us our sins and to cleanse us from all unrighteousness."

What can I change in my life?

What are my goals to achieve it?

Chapter 17

Under Attack

I remember as I was finishing up my book that I was going through a lot of changes the months before completion. Every time I turned around I was under some kind of attack. Seemed like the kids were out of order and they may have been stressed out themselves. There was a high level of stress at my job, and then my body started falling apart. Everything seemed to be going in a constant whirlwind and as a result, it all came crashing down on me. I took a few days off work and it took me about three days just to start feeling the energy that I needed to get out of bed. Every muscle was soar in my body, I felt very fatigued, tired and frustrated. I went to the doctor only to be diagnosed with stress again. This time I was determined not to let stress take over my life. My goal was to complete this book. I also had to balance my everyday life situations. When I took those days off work I began to pray and ask for strength. There were things that needed to be sorted out and accomplished. And all those things were weighing me down...However, some things I had control over so I chose to step back and ignore them just to accomplish my goal of finishing my book. I knew that this was nothing that I wanted to do, but everything that I was destined to do. I knew that someone had to be healed and someone had to hear my story to succeed in their everyday life. Sometimes, we need to restructure our priorities so that we can get our goals accomplished. I know that people are going through struggles and every time that you try to get ahead, there's an obstacle or either pain. On my journey I have learned that the pain never lasts forever and that after pain comes healing. If there is something that you're really trying to accomplish just know that the rollercoaster of life never goes away. You have just got to make your mind up that you are going to see past the distractions. If you really want to see real structure in your life restructure the people in your life. Stand firm on what you believe in and everything else will fall into place. I challenged myself to make sure that I wasn't going to be weighed down with all this stress in the world. I challenged myself to complete my tasks and because of it I was not going to quit. You can't give up when you feel tired and weary. Just refocus, give your time to God, and shut things off from the world. You need that time to be alone with God so that you are in His presence. I needed Him to guide me and to show me where I was struggling. He did that and He removed my stress. If you're ever in a situation and you feel so bugged out that you just want to quit, don't. Just take some time away from everything and everybody and focus your time and attention to God. Let Him talk to you and minister to you so that you gain strength. We can sometimes be overwhelmed and not even know it, but that is when He wants us to turn to Him. He's the only one that can restore all our strength. Continue down your path of faith. You'll be able to look back and know that it was worth every tear, every heartache, and every pain. Make sure that you always are in the will of God so that you can do your assignment effectively and with the right motive. You will begin to realize that your distractions will draw you near to God. Always take time to rest and meditate so that you can hear from God.

MY PRAYER

Dear God,

I come to you asking for peace, strength, and understanding. Let them understand that it is good to get rest and to meditate. Let them understand that their body is a temple and that it needs to be nourished physically and spiritually. Also give them understanding to know that with you all things are possible. Give them the peace that surpasses all understanding so that they may have peace with the decisions that they make. In your son Jesus Christ name we pray,

Amen.

YOUR SCRIPTURE

Psalm 119:15 "I will meditate on your precepts and fix my eyes on your ways."

Matthew 6:34 "Therefore do not be anxious about tomorrow, for tomorrow will be anxious for itself. Sufficient for the day is its own trouble."

John 14:27 "Peace I leave with you; my peace I give to you. Not as the world gives do I give to you. Let not your hearts be troubled, neither let them be afraid."

What can I change in my life?

_____

_____

_____

_____

_____

_____

What are my goals to achieve it?

_____

_____

_____

_____

_____

_____

Chapter 18

Time for yourself

Have you ever thought to yourself "Am I worthy?" "Do I deserve happiness?" "Am I able to be happy?" These are some of the questions that I ask myself daily. I found myself working and taking care of kids and at the same time, I was neglecting myself. I found myself going in stores shopping for my kids when I needed things for myself. I would feel guilty for buying myself a shirt without buying them something. Even though I take care of my kids and they get things more than I do, I still felt guilty. I knew that I was a good mother, but I would still feel guilty when I spent time with myself or bought me something. Whenever I decided that I wanted to have a day at the spa, I usually would take them also. But I am here to tell you that I soon realized that I am worthy of having some "me time". I have also learned that I am not just worthy of love and love from other people, but I am worthy of loving myself and enjoying life. What I realized was that I got caught up in the day-to-day routine that I wasn't enjoying the simple pleasures or living freely. I was merely existing and making others happy. That feeling of being guilty of doing something for myself had to die! I had to realize that if I couldn't take care of myself and pamper myself every now and then I wasn't going to be worth anything to anyone else. This is a very important part of living. If you do the things that you are supposed to do as a mother, as a wife, as a daughter, or a son then you shouldn't feel guilty about doing things for yourself. Also, you must realize that you can't be everything to everybody. It's okay to tell people that you can't do things for them even though you may want to...But at times our body is tired and we can't say "yes" all the time. It's okay to tell people that you can't do it. Taking on a lot of other people's tasks and burdens will drain you. Do not feel guilty for telling someone that you're unable to do things for them. It's not that you're being harsh or being ugly towards them it's to benefit you. You must think about yourself before it's too late. It took me years before I realized this...If you don't find value in yourself, then who? It's important to love yourself, celebrate who you are, and what you mean to others. Don't feel guilty for taking time out to spoil yourself. Look, take yourself out to dinner or to lunch and just enjoy that time alone. God made you in His beautiful image and that alone should make you want to take better care of yourself and not feel guilty for doing it. The amazing thing about God is He puts us through a lot of trials, but always makes us walk out polished and clean. He allows us to find time with Him and during that time He will show you your strengths and weaknesses. As you walk this life's journey know that you're not alone. There are tens and thousands of people that have went through or are going through the same things that you have. But God gives you the strength, courage and endurance to walk through with your head held high and with a perfect smile. He allows you to be able to be a testimony to others so that you can help them along their journey. God also wants you to treat your body as a temple. Carry yourself with courage. Treat yourself with respect and spend quality time with Him. Remember the things that you go through is to make you better not bitter. God wants the most from you. He wants you to be happy and He wants to use your situations to help others. God sent His only son Jesus Christ to die for our sins which was an enormous price. So, the things that we go through could never measure up to the things that Jesus Christ went through for us! You're a beautiful blessing from God. Never give up during any of your circumstances. I used my circumstances to bless you because I know that there is a calling on my life to help others. Let your gifts be a blessing to others and live the best life that you can for God!

MY PRAYER

Dear God,

Thank you for all the many things that you have already blessed us with. Thank you for giving us the wisdom to understand the things that we have been through. Help us to remember that we are your children and that we are worthy of all the blessings that you have for us...and the ones that you will restore. Lord thank you for your command to love and treat others with respect. I pray that everyone understands that every trial that we go through is only a stepping stone and a blessing in disguise. Continue to bless us so that we understand and have the knowledge to be closer and closer to you. You are the reason for everything and you're the reason we live! These and all other blessings in your son Jesus name we pray,

Amen.

YOUR SCRIPTURE

2 Corinthians 9:8 "And God is able to bless you abundantly, so that in all things at all times, having all that you need, you will have abound in every good work."

Isaiah 41:10 "So do not fear, for I am with you, do not be dismayed, for I am your God. I will strengthen you and help you, I will uphold you with my righteous right hand."

Philippians 4:19 "And my God will meet all your needs according to the riches of his glory in Christ Jesus."

John 3:16 "For God so loved the world, that he gave his only son, that whoever believes in him should not perish but have eternal life."

What can I change in my life?

_____

_____

_____

_____

_____

_____

What are my goals to achieve it?

_____

_____

_____

_____

_____

_____

_____

About the Author

Lakesha Denise is a native of Alexander City, AL. She is a graduate of Benjamin Russell High School and has an Associate's Degree in Business Administration from Virginia College of Birmingham. She has two beautiful children, Jada and Trace Trimble. Lakesha Denise is a Motivational Speaker and Life Coach. She boldly shares her testimony of how she learned to have a closer walk with Christ. She teaches others how to depend on the promises of God in their darkest hour even when doubt rises to the surface! Lakesha Denise has overcome the struggles of divorce and single parenting and wants to encourage women and men that they can also move powerfully in their faith!

To book Lakesha Denise for speaking engagements, or to order this book in bulk, send an email to:
Ldt1995@yahoo.com

About the Publisher

Taminko J. Kelley has an MBA in Business Administration from Virginia College. She is a native of Jackson, MS and grew up in a poverty-stricken community called Virden Addition. She is also a graduate of Lanier High School located at 833 W. Maple Street. After 20 years in Corporate America, Taminko was told to leave the building; she was being terminated without any warning. Unknowingly, this knockdown was God's way of escorting her into her destiny. Taminko has always had a love for writing & speaking, so in 2012 God told her to start her own business. Full of uncertainty and with no money, yet by faith, she formed a company called CoolBird Marketing, LLC, which is nestled away in the tiny quaint town of Goodwater, AL. Later she added several other divisions, CoolBird Print Media & Advertising, CoolBird Publishing House, and Taminko J. Kelley & Company.

PO Box 612 | Goodwater, AL 35072
media@coolbirdmarketing.com
www.coolbirdmarketing.com
Toll Free: 888-588-3764

CoolBird
Publishing House
THE AUTHORS NEST

REFERENCE PAGE

Acts 20:35 ESV
1 Chronicles 16:11 KJV
1 Corinthians 15:33 ESV
2 Corinthians 5:7 NIV
2 Corinthians 9:8 NIV
Colossians 3:14 GWT
Corinthians 16:13 NIV
Corinthians 16:14 ESV
Deuteronomy 31:6 NIV
Ephesians 1:17-18 KJV
Genesis 2:24 KJV
Isaiah 40:29 NIV
Isaiah 41:10 NIV
Isaiah 41:10 NIV
Isaiah 41:10 NIV
James 1:12 NASB
James 1:12 NIV
James 1:2-4 NIV
James 3:18 NIV
John 1:9 NIV
John 14:13-14 KJV
John 14:27 ESV
John 14:27 NIV
John 14:27 NIV
John 14:27 NIV
John 14:6 NIV
John 15:7 KJV
John 16:33 NIV

John 3:16 NIV
Joshua 1:9 NIV
Luke 11:9 NIV
Luke 6:38 ESV
Mark 11:24 KJV
Matthew 18:20 KJV
Matthew 1819 KJV
Matthew 19:6 NKJV
Matthew 5:16 NIV
Matthew 6:34 ESV
1 Peter 3:9 NIV
1 Peter 5:6 NIV
1 Peter 5:7 NIV
1 Peter 5:7 NIV
1 Peter 5:7 NIV
Philippians 4:13 NKJV
Philippians 4:19 NIV
Philippians 4:19 NIV
Philippians 4:6-7 NIV
Philippians 4:7 NIV
Proverbs 11:25 ESV
Proverbs 19:21 ESV
Proverbs 22:6 NIV
Proverbs 3:5 ESV
Proverbs 3:5-6 NIV
Psalm 138: 8 ESV
Psalm 107 28-30 KJV
Psalm 119: 71 NIV

Psalm 119:130 NIV
Psalm 119:15 ESV
Psalm 120:1 NIV
Psalm 37:8 ESZV
Psalm 51:10- 12 NIV
Psalm 56:3 NIV
Psalm 56:3 NIV
Psalm 86: 1 NIV
Psalm 9:165 NIV
Psalm 9:18 NIV
Romans 12: 13 ESV
Romans 12: 21 NKJV
Romans 12:12 NIV
Romans 12:8 NIV
Romans 14:19 NIV
Romans 15:1 KJV
Romans 2:6 NIV
Romans 2:6 NIV
Romans 5:3 NIV
Romans 8: 28 ESV
Romans 8:28 KJV
Romans 8:28 NIV
1 Timothy 2:5 NIV

Made in the USA
Columbia, SC
17 May 2021